God Bless You,
James T. Draper, Jr.
Rom. 1:16

Say Neighbor -
Your House is on Fire!

Say Neighbor -
Your House is on Fire!

by
James T. Draper Jr.

**with foreword by
Cliff Barrows**

CRESCENDO BOOK PUBLICATIONS
DALLAS, TEXAS

Say Neighbor - Your House is on Fire!

by James T. Draper, Jr.

COPYRIGHT © 1975

CRESCENDO BOOK PUBLICATIONS
DALLAS, TEXAS

ISBN: 0-89038-021-X

Library of Congress Catalog Card Number: 75-6207

Printed in the United States of America

**Dedication to
My Christian Parentage**

My Grandfather, L.M. Keeling,
who preached for 54 years,

My Father, James T. Draper,
who preached for 36 years,

My Grandmother, Pearl Compton Keeling,
and My Mother, Lois Keeling Draper,
*who stood by their preacher-husbands
in a way to cause Heaven to rejoice.*

The examples of these saints of the Lord have been
used to strengthen, encourage and bless my life in
countless ways. To them, these pages are dedicated.

FOREWORD

WHAT WOULD YOU DO
IF YOUR NEIGHBOR'S HOUSE WERE ON FIRE?...

Just what Jimmy Draper did, probably, but 999 out of 1,000 of us have never really seen our neighbor's house on fire.... That is, unless we have looked with spiritual eyes which only God can give us.

The parallel that the author draws from his own personal experience can be a lesson to each one of us. *There is something we can do*, and this unique volume of "warning messages" from the heart and pen of a man who knows God and who loves to preach His Word will inspire us to do it.

May the "fire in our neighbor's house" become a consuming flame in our own soul that will purify and propel us through the power of the Holy Spirit to "rescue the perishing and care for the dying."

During the time of our fellowship together in Dallas, I came to know Jimmy as a man with a pastor's heart and a genuine love for people. These qualities, combined with his knowledge of the Bible, are reflected in the messages that follow in this book—"Say, Neighbor, Your House is on Fire!"

Cliff Barrows

Table of Contents

CHAPTER I

Say Neighbor,
Your House Is On Fire!

The night was crisp and crystal clear and the stars brilliantly stood out against the blackened sky. My wife, Carol Ann, and I were returning from a late time of fellowship with Cliff and Billie Barrows, Gil and Ann Stricklin, and Millie Kohn. We had met at the Stricklin's home for a light meal following crusade services in our church. The Barrows and Millie left around midnight and we began to leave with them. Gil insisted that we stay and visit as we had had such little time for fellowship since coming to Dallas. Finally, Carol Ann and I left the Stricklin's home around 1:00 a.m. We headed for home enjoying the beauty of the night and reflecting on the warmth and joy of fellowship with friends. As we topped the hill a mile or so south of our home we saw flames leaping from the roof of a house near ours. I sped up and hurried to the sight of the fire. I fully expected to see fire trucks, policemen and many bystanders. Instead I found a deserted street and my neighbor's house in full blaze.

When we arrived on the scene, I jumped from the car and ran to the front door and began to pound on the door to see if anyone was home. The fire had started in the garage and worked its way into the house. My neighbors were all sleeping in the area of the home that was farthest from the fire. Because of this the fire was in unbridled fury and at the height of its destructive force before the smoke became a problem for them in the other extreme of the building. By the time I reached the front door, the only safe avenue of escape was through that front door. The rear of the home was engulfed in flames. The windows were not conducive for escape. Their only hope was through the front door.

Shortly after I began to pound on the door, I could see the forms of two small children through the opaque glass in the front door. I urged them to unlock the door. They tried, but the locks were too difficult for their tender hands. Quickly I leaned back and tried to kick the door down. To my horror, the solid-core door was solid indeed! As I began to contemplate what to do since I could not kick open the door, another form appeared in the small opaque glass of the door. It was the eldest daughter and she managed to get the three locks (one at the top, one in the middle, and one in the bottom of the door) unlocked and the door flew open.

When the door came open smoke belched from the house like smoke from the end of a shotgun following firing. It was asphyxiating, smothering, suffocating smoke. The heat and fury of the burning home made the smoke unbearable. No one could have survived long in it. Already the smoke hung down to within eighteen inches of the floor. A few more minutes and my neighbors would have been dead. I entered the home briefly to lead the mother from the home and then arranged for them to stay elsewhere for the night.

The spiritual implications of the experience have staggered me. The first and obvious thing was that God led me to come by at just the right time. Had I been earlier or later, my neighbors would have died. He led me to be there at just the needed moment. The leading of the Holy Spirit was so obvious. He had also led me to change clothes before going to the Stricklin's even though Gil and Cliff were in business suits. I felt I should change, and did so, not knowing until later why I should do so. I rose to leave for home at least six times before I did leave. Now I see that God had a precise moment He wanted me to leave. Neighbors two doors from the fire had been outside fifteen minutes earlier and had not seen the fire as it was then contained in its beginning stages. He brought me there at just the proper time. God's timing is always perfect.

The next thing that stands out in my mind is that by the time I reached the home there was but one way of escape. The house burned in such a way that the only way of safe escape was through the front door. I woke the family up and warned them of the danger. But I could not knock the door down. I could only warn them. They lived because they responded to my warning and opened the door from the inside. You can readily see the spiritual implications of that. There is only one avenue of escape for mankind. That way is Jesus Christ. Mankind needs to be warned of the doom and danger that lurks ahead. But no one can force another to receive Christ. Each man, in God's precise timing, must open the door of his heart from the inside if he is to live. My neighbors are alive today because they heeded my warning and opened the door from the inside.

Nothing so devastates a house like fire. No one likes his house to burn. No one desires his house to burn. Fire is always an unwelcomed invader of the sanctity of a household. In fact, elaborate precautions are built into every well-planned house to prevent fires, since all the plans, dreams and anticipations for the house are tragically destroyed when a fire strikes.

Life is not unlike that. Every man has his dreams, his goals, his plans for his life. Happiness and satisfaction are sought as worthy goals. Each man works toward a goal of independence and contentment. That is his "dream house." How tragic it is when that dream house is destroyed. How desperate it is when such dreams are destroyed and hopes are dashed to pieces as life crumbles in a person's hands. Every one's life contains the latent beginnings of fire. Inherently each person has tendencies toward self-destruction. The pages of this book concern these tendencies. In addition, they contain God's warnings about those tendencies as well as the possibility for realization of life's greatest dreams.

Man's Perilous Condition

Every person is in danger of disaster. The Bible says, "The heart is deceitful above all things, and desperately wicked: who can know it?" (Jeremiah 17:9). Within the heart of every person exists a desperate wickedness. Man's heart is filled with every conceivable kind of evil. All the concentrated evil of hell itself resides within the heart of every man. There is no crime man will not commit. There is no rebellion too vulgar for his life. There is no limiting his lust. There is no curbing his passion. There is no satisfying his greed. Man's sensuous heart has created a perilous condition for every person. Jesus said, "Those things which proceed out of the mouth come forth from the heart; and they defile the man. For out of the heart proceed evil thoughts, murders, adulteries, fornications, thefts, false witness, blasphemies: these are the things which defile a man" (Matthew 15:18-20). Another reference asserts, "That which cometh out of the man, that defileth the man. For from within, out of the heart of man, proceed evil thoughts, adulteries, fornications, murders, thefts, covetousness, wickedness, deceit, lasciviousness, an evil eye, blasphemy, pride, foolishness: all these evil things come from within, and defile the man'' (Mark 7: 20-23). Still another statement charges, ''An evil man out of the evil treasure of his heart bringeth forth that which is evil: for of the abundance of the heart his mouth speaketh'' (Luke 6:45). Man's wicked heart is capable of producing every conceivable evil.

This condition becomes more critical when we realize that its viciousness and rebellion is directed against God. Man's heart does not rail against other men. It rails against God. David cried out, ''I acknowledge my transgression: and my sin is ever before me. Against thee, thee only, have I sinned, and done this evil in thy sight'' (Psalm 51:3-4). Though he had abdicated his position as king, failing the nation drastically and dramatically, and though he had destroyed the family of Uriah, he had deliberately and specifically sinned against God. In the New Testament, the prodigal son had disgraced his family and dissipated his life. When he came home to his disappointed and heart-broken father, he cried, ''Father, I have sinned against heaven, and in thy sight'' (Luke 15:21). He acknowledged that his sin was basically an act of rebellion against God, although it was committed in the presence of man.

Such lust in the heart is far-reaching in its distribution and in its consequences. The Apostle Paul wrote, ''There is none righteous, no, not one: there is none that understandeth, there is none that seeketh after God. They are all gone out of the way, they are together become unprofitable; there is none that doeth good, no, not one. Their throat is an open sepulchre; with their tongues they have used deceit; the poison of asps is under their lips: whose mouth is full of cursing and bitterness: their feet are swift to shed blood: destruction and misery are in their ways: and the way of peace have they not known: there is no fear of God before their eyes. The wages of sin is death" (Romans 3:10-18; 6:23). The writer of Proverbs asserts that "at the last it biteth like a serpent, and stingeth like an adder" (Proverbs 23:32). The Apostle James says, "When lust hath conceived, it bringeth forth sin: and sin, when it is finished, bringeth forth death" (James 1:15). The end result of sin is frightening! The ancient prophet declared, "The soul that sinneth it shall die" (Ezekiel 18:4). Even back in the Garden of Eden God revealed to Adam, "Of every tree of the garden thou mayest freely eat: but of the tree of the knowledge of good and evil, thou shalt not eat of it: for in the day that thou eatest thereof thou shalt surely die" (Genesis 2:16-17). In Romans 5:12 we are told the results of Adam's rebellion.

Man's fatal tendency toward sin has brought him to great danger. Every man's "house" is in flames. His condition is perilous. We stand in danger of judgment and hell. We cannot survive without outside intervention. None but God has the compassion to warn us, and the power to rescue us from our peril and the wisdom to restore us to safety. Man's only hope is to heed God's warning and to appropriate His provision.

God's Continual Warning

The extreme concern of God is seen in the great lengths He has gone to warn man of his peril. He did not warn us by some celestial display or the stunning signs of nature. Nor did He do it by the moving words of poetic beauty or stirring tunes of angelic harmony. He did not select the simple words of rhetoric or profound utterance to warn man. He warned man by the Word, even His only begotten Son. His call of warning was the eternal, incarnate Son of God—Jesus Christ. He sent His Son to fill with meaning and understanding the biblical revelation and thus through Him to appeal to the hearts of men. How much does God love us? How deep is His concern?

How incessant are His warnings to the hearts of men? They are limitless in their scope and never-ending in their frequency.

God's warnings to men stand out like bold mountain peaks in the Word of God. Emblazened in the Word, they leap forth from page after page of the divine revelation. At creation God warned Adam of the danger of disobedience (Genesis 2:17). From that time onward, God has never ceased to warn man. To wicked Cain, God warned, "If thou doest not well, sin lieth at the door" (Genesis 4:7). When man began to multiply in the earth, his heart began to be filled with wickedness continually, and God warned, "My spirit shall not always strive with man" (Genesis 6:3). Even the patience and longsuffering of God had its limits. Beware, sin lies at every man's door and only awaits the opportunity to destroy him and his dreams.

God even warned Pharaoh before pronouncing judgment on him. Then in the wilderness the wandering Israelites rebelled and God warned Moses, "I have seen this people, and, behold, it is a stiffnecked people: now therefore let me alone, that my wrath may wax hot against them, and that I may consume them" (Exodus 32:9-10). God's warnings of impending judgment are everywhere seen in the Word of God. When two of the tribes of Israel considered refusing to do God's command, God sternly warned, "If ye will not do so, behold, ye have sinned against the Lord: and be sure your sin will find you out" (Numbers 32:23). Sin will always reveal itself. It will always be discovered. Sin is always exposed and judged. God warns us that such is the truth. He also warns us that His patience does come to an end and His justice intervenes.

The Psalmist reminded the Israelites, "The Lord knoweth the way of the righteous: but the way of the ungodly shall perish" (Psalm 1:6). Again he wrote, "The

Lord is known by the judgment which he executeth: the wicked is snared in the work of his own hands. The wicked shall be turned into hell, and all the nations that forget God" (Psalm 9:16-17). Consistently God warns man that the wicked will not go unpunished and that His grace and longsuffering has an end to its patience.

Throughout the Old Testament, the prophets pronounced sober warnings against sin. God declared through Amos, "I have overthrown some of you, as God overthrew Sodom and Gomorrah, and ye were as a firebrand plucked out of the burning: yet have ye not returned unto me, saith the Lord. Therefore thus will I do unto thee, O Israel: and because I will do this unto thee, prepare to meet thy God, O Israel" (Amos 4:11-12). Israel's rejection and rebellion against her God would surely result in judgmental confrontation between Israel and Jehovah God.

Always coupled with God's warnings are the promises of forgiveness and salvation. Man's response to God's warnings is the key. For example, four times in Amos' prophecy in chapter five is the admonition, "See ye me, and ye shall live." Always God's warnings are for the purpose of bestowing life and blessing if man responds. The prophet Malachi wrote "For behold, the day cometh, that shall burn as an oven; and all the proud, yea, and all that do wickedly, shall be stubble: and the day that cometh shall burn them up, saith the Lord of hosts, that it shall leave them neither root nor branch. But unto you that fear my name shall the Son of righteousness arise with healing in his wings; and ye shall go forth, and grow up as calves of the stall. And ye shall tread down the wicked; for they shall be ashes under the soles of your feet in the day that I shall do this, saith the Lord of hosts. Remember ye the law of Moses my servant, which I commanded unto him the Horeb for all Israel, with the statues and judgments. Behold, I will send you Elijah the prophet before the coming of the great and dreadful day of the

Lord: and he shall turn the heart of the fathers to the children, and the heart of the children to their fathers, lest I come and smite the earth with a curse" (Malachi 4:1-6). Nowhere in the writings of the prophets is God's warning, forgiveness and firmness in judgment more clearly seen than in these closing words of the Old Testament.

Our Lord Jesus Christ underscored the attitude of Almighty God toward man's sin and disobedience. He said, "He that is not with me is against me; and he that gathereth not with me scattereth abroad. Wherefore I say unto you, All manner of sin and blasphemy shall be forgiven unto men: but the blasphemy against the Holy Ghost shall not be forgiven unto men. And whosoever speaketh a word against the Son of man, it shall be forgiven him: but whosoever speaketh against the Holy Ghost, it shall not be forgiven him, neither in this world, neither in the world to come. Every idle word that men shall speak, they shall give account thereof in the day of judgment" (Matthew 12:30-32, 36). How poignant and penetrating are the warnings of our God!

The writer of Hebrews presents to us one of the most revealing words of warning to be found anywhere in the Bible. He asserts, "It is impossible for those who were once enlightened, and have tasted of the heavenly gift, and were made partakers of the Holy Ghost, and have tasted the good word of God, and the powers of the world to come, if they shall fall away to renew them again unto repentance; seeing they crucify to themselves the Son of God afresh, and put him to an open shame. For if we sin wilfully after that we have received the knowledge of the truth, there remaineth no more sacrifice for sins, but a certain fearful looking for of judgment and fiery indignation, which shall devour the adversaries" (Hebrews 6:4-6; 10:26-27). Certain lines of conduct call for severe means of judgment and punishment from God. God continually warns us of impending judgment to rebellious hearts.

The Apostle Paul, in his First Corinthian letter, spoke of the Judgment Seat of Christ which awaits every Christian. His warning is a reminder to us to utilize every opportunity to the glory of the Lord. It calls us to a quality of life and service that will meet with reward and not rebuke in that day. He wrote, "For other foundation can no man lay than that is laid, which is Jesus Christ. Now if any man build upon this foundation gold, silver, precious stones, wood, hay, stubble; every man's work shall be made manifest: for the day shall declare it, because it shall be revealed by fire; and the fire shall try every man's work of what sort it is. If any man's work abide which he hath built thereupon, he shall receive a reward. If any man's work shall be burned, he shall suffer loss: but he himself shall be saved; yet so as by fire. Know ye not that ye are the temple of God, and that the Spirit of God dwelleth in you? If any man defile the temple of God, him shall God destroy; for the temple of God is holy, which temple ye are" (I Corinthians 3:11-17). His warning is for believers. We, too must stand in judgment for the deeds we do in the flesh.

The closing chapters of the Book of the Revelation find God issuing stern warning of eternal judgment to those who reject Him. The beloved Apostle John said, "And I saw a great white throne, and him that sat on it, from whose face the earth and the heaven fled away; and there was found no place for them. And I saw the dead, small and great, stand before God; and the books were opened: and another book was opened, which is the book of life: and the dead were judged out of these things which were written in the books, according to their works. And the sea gave up the dead which were in it; and death and hell delivered up the dead which were in them: and they were judged every man according to their works. And death and hell were cast into the lake of fire. This is the second death. And whosoever was not found written in the book of life was cast into the lake of fire" (Revelation 20:11-15). Unbelievers are here placed in judgment for the deeds done in the flesh. From Genesis through Revelation, God continually and consistently warns man of the tragedy of rejection and rebellion. His warning of impending judgment of sin and rebellion constantly remind us that we are accountable for the way we live.

God's Response to Man's Commitment

Nevertheless, the warnings of God always include a call to repentance and a promise of blessing. God always gives previous provision to man's heart when he responds to the warnings of impending judgment for sin. The Psalmist noted God's response to man's commitment when he declared, "Trust in the Lord, and do good; so shalt thou dwell in the land, and verily thou shalt be fed. Delight thyself also in the Lord; and he shall give thee the desires of thine heart. Commit thy way unto the Lord; trust also in him; and he shall bring it to pass. Fret not thyself in any wise to do evil. For evildoers shall be cut off: but those that wait upon the Lord, they shall inherit the earth. The meek shall inherit the earth; and shall delight themselves in the abundance of peace. The Lord upholdeth the righteous. The Lord knoweth the days of the upright: and their inheritance shall be for ever (Psalm 37: 3-5, 8-9, 11, 17-18). God always responds to repentance and genuine commitment to Himself. His love reaches us in gracious provision when we acknowledge our rebellion and seek His forgiveness.

So firm is the response of God, that nothing can happen to us that will remove us from His provision for our lives once we have committed our lives to Him. He responds in an almost unbelievable and eternal provision for our needs. He assures us that "We know that all things work together for good to them that love God, to them who are the called according to his purpose. If God be for us, who

24

can be against us? Who shall separate us from the love of Christ? Shall tribulation, or distress, or persecution, or famine, or nakedness, or peril, or sword? Nay, in all these things we are more than conquerors through Him that loved us. For I am persuaded, that neither death, nor life, nor angels, nor principalities, nor powers, nor things present, nor things to come, nor height, nor depth, nor any other creature, shall be able to separate us from the love of God, which is in Christ Jesus our Lord" (Romans 8:28, 31, 35, 37-39).

Eternal life, assurance of salvation, freedom from guilt, joy in service, satisfaction and confidence in daily living—all these come through our response to God's warnings for our lives. His warnings are always engulfed in His love. He warns only because He loves us and longs to have perfect fellowship with us through all eternity. How much we need to respond to God's continual call to our hearts.

As we respond to Him, we can look toward the future with joy and anticipation. With excitement we greet the words, "For the Lord himself shall descend from heaven with a shout, with the voice of the archangel, and with the trump of God: and the dead in Christ shall rise first: then we which are alive and remain shall be caught up together with them in the clouds to meet the Lord in the air: and so shall we ever be with the Lord" (I Thessalonians 4:16-17). Such delight in His return can only come to those who have responded in faith and repentance to the warnings of God. For those who so respond, the closing words of the Word of God have great meaning: "And the Spirit and the bride say, Come. And let him that heareth say, Come. And let him that is athirst come. And whosoever will, let him him take the water of life freely" (Revelation 22:17). When we come as He has urged us, we can greet His promise, "Surely I come quickly," with the response of a grateful and forgiven heart, "Amen. Even so, come, Lord Jesus" (Revelation 22:20).

Men and women around the world today need to be warned of impending doom and judgment. We can and must warn them. They can and must open the door inside their hearts if they are to live. I do not debate whether or not to warn men and women of spiritual disaster. I must do it.

This volume is an attempt to present some of the warning messages of the Bible in such a way that men and women may hear God's warning and open the door of their hearts and be saved. If these pages can help one person open the door, I rejoice. If they can help another Christian verbalize God's warnings in such a way as to lead others to the Saviour, I shall doubly rejoice. The title is borne out of this warning experience in my own neighborhood: "Say, Neighbor, Your House Is On Fire!" May we be evangels of the warning messages of God to the neighborhoods of our world.

CHAPTER II

Lonely Voices

In the beginning when God created man, He paused to say, "It is good." Then God said, "It is not good for man to be alone" (Genesis 2:18). So God created for Adam a companion, someone to be with him. Loneliness was the first thing God said was not good in this world. Today we have come to a terrific paradox, a contradiction, for there is a great deal of difference between being alone and being lonely. We can hardly ever be alone. We would like to be alone on some occasions. We are often with one another more than we would like to be. Sometimes it appears that there is no way to get alone.

But the tragedy of our century is that although we are in the midst of millions of people, we are lonely. Our number one problem is loneliness. The truth is that loneliness has nothing to do with quantity. We may be in a crowd and still be lonely. Man is a social being. He was not created to live alone or in loneliness. When the heart of man reaches out for companionship and fellowship and does not find it, it experiences one of the saddest things that can happen in an individual's life.

Now the Bible speaks of this. There are many instances where the Word of God speaks of loneliness. For instance, the Psalmist cried out to God saying, "For my days are consumed like smoke and my bones are burned as an hearth; my heart is smitten and withered like grass so that I forget to eat my bread" (Psalm 102:3-4). His heart was so lonely and he felt so utterly forsaken that he was not hungry. He could not even remember to eat. "I am like a pelican of the wilderness: I am like an owl of the desert. I watch, and am as a sparrow alone upon the house top" (Psalm 102:6-7). Utterly and completely alone he awaited the inevitable. "My days are like a shadow that declineth; and I am withered like grass" (Psalms 102:11). What a tragic picture. It portrays someone utterly forsaken, alone and lonely. I do not think this is an exaggeration of our condition today, because I find that the majority of those with whom I counsel are people who face this problem of loneliness.

That loneliness may have come as the result of a divorce, a death, an estrangement, or some other lack of communication. Though surrounded by people, the real cry of the heart is, "I don't want to be alone. I don't want to be lonely. I need someone." I want to address this matter by describing loneliness and by indicating some false ways that we try to cure loneliness. The Psalmist declared, "I cried unto the Lord with my voice; with my voice unto the Lord did I make my supplication. I poured out my complaint before him; I shewed him my trouble. When my spirit was overwhelmed within me, then thou knewest my path. In the way wherein I walked have they privily laid a snare for me. I looked on my right hand, and beheld, but there was no man that would know me: refuge failed me; no man cared for my soul" (Psalm 142:1-4).

Oh, what a tragic cry that is: "No one cared for my soul." I do not know how often people say, "No one cares about me. I am forsaken. I am alone. No one cares what happens to me." The tragedy of that mentality and the tragedy of that complaint is that it is often not true. In the

Old Testament, the prophet Elijah thought he was forsaken too. He ran off into the wilderness. When God came to him to get him to reveal the problem, he said, "I am alone. Not anybody in the whole world loves you but me." God replied, "I have left me seven thousand in Israel, all the knees which have not bowed unto Baal, and every mouth which hath not kissed him" (I Kings 19:18). The prophet had exaggerated the situation. He thought he was alone. He thought no one cared. He thought there was no interest in God or in the things of God. He was concerned, but he was wrong. That is why it is very dangerous for us to allow Satan to exaggerate our feelings and emotions. That is why we should stand upon the Word of God and let it govern our actions. We need to realize that our feelings will betray us. Our emotions are fickle. We need to stand solidly upon the Word of God for our strength and for our direction in life.

Characteristics of Loneliness

Let me describe loneliness to you. There are three basic characteristics of loneliness that are seen in Psalm 142. Although it was written centuries ago, it is applicable for today. These characteristics describe our lives and our problems today.

The first characteristic of loneliness is alienation. This occurs when we feel cut off. We feel alienated from those around us and we get a sense of loneliness. It often occurs when our circumstances change and we feel we have lost a common bond, a common tie with friends and things we once knew. That is what the Psalmist says, "I looked on my right hand, and beheld, but there was no man that would know me" (Psalm 142:4). He felt cut off and alienated. He felt as if he had been imprisoned.

It is interesting that those who study contemporary American society describe many of our living complexes as prisons. Theodore Vandellen, in a copyrighted story syndicated in *The Chicago Tribune* and *The New York Times* said, "Many high rises are like prisons, and people who live in them tend to be inadequate and indifferent." If you think that is a minor problem, an article in the *Dallas Times Herald* stated that currently 27% of all of the new residential construction throughout the nation was in high-rise apartments and condominium buildings. Such buildings are described by their occupants as prisons. "We are cut off. We are separated. We are alienated," they say. "Although we are surrounded by all these people, we are forsaken. We are alone." The first characteristic of loneliness is alienation.

A second characteristic of loneliness is frustration. We see it in our text, "I looked on my right hand, and beheld, but there was no man that would know me: refuge failed me; no man cared for my soul" (Psalm 142:4). Can you imagine any more frustration than that? Everywhere I turned, I failed. To make matters worse, everyone turned their backs upon me. Nobody cares for my soul. He was experiencing the frustration of not belonging, of emptiness of not having anyone to please, purposelessness. It is like playing golf alone. When you do well, hit a good shot or make a great putt, there is no one with whom to share it. It is an impossible situation. That is the frustration of people in our society who are lonely. There is a basic frustration and sense of purposelessness.

Harold Lovotsky of Northwestern University recently made this comment: "The emptiness of the decade of the 1950's became boredom, then it became futility and now it is despair. But this is to be expected because an individual cannot live in a condition of emptiness for very long." We cannot survive for long if we have no reason to live, nothing for which to work, no one to please, no one to help. We are only a step away from a mental institution or the graveyard. We cannot survive very long in such a vacuum. It develops in us a sense of futility and frustration. What a tragic characteristic of loneliness.

A third characteristic of loneliness is depression. The Psalmist says, "My spirit was overwhelmed with me" (Psalms 142:3). The word "depression" means "pressed down." It indicates that something is under strain or stress. It means to be overwhelmed. Professor Lovotsky went on to say, "There are more cases of depression being seen today than ever before. Once depression becomes the response to stress, it will continue to be the response to stress throughout life." Boredom and depression in a computer age, is that not strange? In a push-button age with all our modern conveniences, the number one problem facing our world is depression. Are you depressed? Well, you are going to live with it the rest of your life, unless something happens to take care of that depression. Depression is a characteristic of loneliness and if depression is your reaction to those things, you are going to react that way all of your life.

Depression came upon Judas when his betrayal of Jesus Christ began to weigh upon him and he realized that he had betrayed an innocent person. He could not stand the thought of what he had done, so he committed suicide. There is a rise in suicide in our day. We are told that suicide attempts always come after crises experiences. Depression is brought on by failure, broken relationships and crisis experiences.

How do you react to these things? Now be honest, because I want to tell you that there is an answer. We do not have to be depressed. We do not have to go through life alienated, frustrated and depressed. We do not have to do it. If we do, it is our own choosing. God does not want us to do it. He wants us to experience joy, fulfillment and fellowship. The characteristics of alienation, frustration and depression are common in our society today, but they need not be ours.

False Cures for Loneliness

There are some false ways that people try to cure their loneliness. I wish I could go into them in detail with you, but space permits me only to briefly mention four false ways Satan tries to tell us how to overcome loneliness. Anything Satan gives us is counterfeit at the outset, so we are already forewarned. Everything Satan tells us is like the cigarette advertisement that says, "It satisfies." What a lie that is! If it satisfied, only one would be needed. It does not satisfy, it merely whets our appetite until it binds us to a habit. Satan lies to us like that. He tells us that one thing will make us happy and then he points us on to the next thrill or experience. As we move along his way, we find it only keeps us going and going and going. There are false ways that Satan tries to tell us will cure loneliness, but they are merely lures and not cures at all.

One such suggestion as a cure for loneliness is drugs. Drugs are counterfeit from the start. They will not work to cure loneliness because drugs always leave us depressed. It matters not how high we go, we have to come down again. Those who push and promote drugs admit that drugs cause halucinations. Any way we describe halucination we find it to be an artificial experience. It is not genuine. It is counterfeit. I cannot understand why anyone would be satisfied with something artificial when they could have the real thing. I cannot fathom why anyone would chose to attempt to warm themselves by a picture, an artificial representation of a fire, rather than warming themselves by a genuine fire that gives real warmth.

Now you say, "Why are you so against drugs?" I can tell you in a nutshell why I am against drugs. Whether it be alcohol or narcotics of any kind, it distorts the image of God within me. Since this image of God is my rational ability to understand truth and to relate to God and my fellow man to think and to love, I do not want to distort its ability to relate accurately. Under the influence of any kind of narcotic, I immediately find that the image of God which allows me to think, to love, to respond, is damaged. Drugs go straight to what is like God in us. One drink, one pill, one shot, or one dose, however administered, attacks God in us. It is just like that. Drugs are tragic and counterfeit because they distort the image of God in us and leave us depressed.

A second way Satan suggests that we cure loneliness is by means of sex. It is difficult to believe the kind of society in which we live. There are many in our society who practice promiscuous sex as a way of life. Let me tell you why sex will not work as a cure for loneliness. While drugs leave us depressed, sex leaves us guilty. Satan's solution for loneliness is false. Sometime back two baseball players swapped wives and families. I thought that was an amazing thing. How strange it seemed to me. But I have discovered in these past months that that is not strange at all. There are indeed many, many thousands of people who practice mate-swapping week in and week out in their effort to find meaning, satisfaction, pleasure and purpose in life. It is a perverted, counterfeit attempt to satisfy the loneliness of the heart. The result of such promiscuity is always guilt.

A third way Satan suggests that we overcome loneliness is by hostility. Lonely people are basically hostile people. We might hear someone say, "I do not have a wife, so I am mad at everybody who does." If a particular thing seems to be a problem to us, we look for it in everybody else. We get hostile about it and attack it in others. Let me tell you something about the criticism and gossip that stems from such hostility. The people who gossip open their souls when they speak because the thing they criticize is the thing that is their own weakness. When somebody begins to criticize a certain thing in the lives of others, we can be sure that it is their problem. If a gossip wants the whole world to know what he or she is like, they should just continue to criticize and gossip. Did you ever wonder why hostility is a false cure for loneliness? It is a false cure because hostility always leaves us bitter. Drugs leave us depressed. Sex leaves us guilty. Hostility leaves us bitter at the world. They are all false cures for loneliness.

Still another false cure for loneliness is increased religious activity. The reason increased activity does not satisfy is that it is frenzied and it always leaves us empty. The emptiest I have ever been as a minister of the gospel, are those periods in my life when I became so busy that I did not take time to get alone with God. I did not take time to study like I should, and I did not take time to be on my face before God. Whenever I got into such a condition, I was empty. Just as we can only pour so much water out of a glass before we have got to fill it up again, so we must be refilled in our work for God. Increased, frenzied activity leaves us empty. It is one of Satan's false cures for loneliness. We need to spend time alone with God to be so filled.

The Cure for Loneliness

What, then, is the cure for loneliness? I can tell you in a word—"fellowship." After the Psalmist described his terrible state of depression, frustration and alienation, he said, "I cried unto them O Lord: I said, Thou art my refuge" (Psalm 142:5). God was his salvation. He was his refuge in troublesome times. This fellowship is not fellowship with just anybody. It is fellowship with God through Christ. Christ is to be in us and we are to be in Christ. He is the One who made us. He is the One who knows what makes us happy. He is the One who understands our needs. Fellowship with Him, that is the primary ingredient in the real cure for loneliness.

Along with fellowship is worship. Worship is a cure for loneliness. The Psalmist says, "Bring my soul out of prison, that I may praise thy name: the righteous shall compass me about: for thou shalt deal bountifully with me" (Psalm 142:7). When we praise God, we worship Him. Then we "Enter into his gates with thanksgiving, and into his courts with praise" (Psalm 100:4). Praise is worship. If we want to be cured from loneliness, we need to commit ourselves to Jesus Christ, and then bow down and worship Him both publicly and privately.

Perhaps I should put it one other way. Really, the cure for loneliness is finding and maintaining a relationship with God. We stop being lonely when we become involved with someone else. The real cure for loneliness, however, is not a relationship with just any person. It is a relationship with Jesus Christ, the only real person who has ever lived. He is the only man who walked this way and faced all of the temptations I face, yet He is without sin. He is the only man who looked Satan in the eye and cast him down and buried him underneath the cross. We need a relationship with Him—Jesus Christ. That is why Paul could rejoice in prison. In his epistle to the church at Philippi he said, "Rejoice" or some companion word over forty times. You see, the reason he was not lonely in prison was that he was a prisoner of Christ. He was bound to Jesus. He had a personal relationship with Jesus Christ who said, "I will never leave thee, nor forsake thee" (Hebrews 13:5). We are never alone if Christ is in our hearts. That is what the Psalmist was declaring in the twenty-third Psalm, "The Lord is my shepherd; I shall not want" (Psalm 23:1).

Loneliness is the result of our own choosing. It is the result of our own attitude. It is the result of our attitude that rebels against God. When we push God out of our lives, we alienate ourselves from Him. We choose to be lonely. We ought not cry about how lonely we are if, when we know the truth, we push it away. The cure to loneliness is to bow our knees before Christ. We need not change our circumstances. We need to change ourselves. Jesus Christ will create a new heart, a new life, a new outlook, a new purpose, a new direction for our lives if we will but let Him. That is the real cure for loneliness.

That cure is available to each one of us. We do not have to go searching for it. The Word of God is near us, even in our mouths and in our hearts, if we would but call upon Him. We do not have to go up into heaven to search for it, nor dive into the depths of the sea to seek it. Nor do we need to go around the world to draw it into our hearts. The Word of God is available to all of us. It is at the door of our hearts. As the Apostle Paul wrote, "The word is nigh thee, even in thy mouth, and in thy heart: that is, the word of faith, which we preach; that if thou shalt confess with thy mouth the Lord Jesus, and shalt believe in thine heart that God hath raised him from the dead, thou shalt be saved. For with the heart man believeth unto righteousness; and with the mouth confession is made unto salvation. For whosoever shall call upon the name of the Lord shall be saved" (Romans 10:8-10, 13).

We can be saved not only from our sins, not only from hell, but from ourselves and from our loneliness. The choice is ours. Christ is the answer. We need to have a relationship with Him. I am not saying, "If you commit yourself to Christ, all of a sudden everything you want will come to you." I am saying, "If you never find a change in your circumstances, a commitment to Christ says to Him, 'I am willing to be like this the rest of my life, if it brings honor to you.' " A commitment like that will bring God's best to us. It will change us in the midst of our circumstances and give us grace to sustain us in our distress. Then we can say with Paul, "I begged God to make me well again. Each time he said, 'No. But I am with you; that is all you need. My power shows up best in weak people.' Now I am glad to boast about how weak I am; I am glad to be a living demonstration of Christ's power, instead of showing off my own power and abilities" (II Corinthians 12:8-9—*Living Bible*). We can come to God like that if we are willing for Him to work a miracle in our lives. Loneliness? That is just a word in the dictionary. It need not be in our experience because Christ is there. He is the cure for all of our needs—including loneliness.

CHAPTER III

Sealed and Secured

Nothing so destroys spiritual joy and vitality like doubt. The Word of God speaks often concerning the dispelling of doubt and the removal of doubt. Nowhere is the security of the soul so underscored as in the doctrine of the "sealing" of the Holy Spirit. Properly understood this truth will cast away doubt and cause us to rejoice in the confidence of God. Many people think you are going to speak of the Spirit-filled life when you mention being sealed with the Spirit. To be sealed with the Spirit is not the same thing as being filled with the Spirit or controlled by the Spirit. The Apostle Paul speaks of being sealed with the Spirit when he writes, "In whom ye also trusted, after that ye heard the word of truth, the gospel of your salvation: in whom also after that ye believed, ye were sealed with that Holy Spirit of promise, which is the earnest of our inheritance until the redemption of the purchased possession, unto the praise of his glory" (Ephesians 1:13-14). He declares, "Ye were sealed." That is a very clear and positive statement. It is hard to get around, spiritualize or explain it away. It is a powerful statement. After you heard the gospel, he says, you believed and when you believed you were sealed with the Spirit of God.

When speaking about being sealed with the Holy Spirit of God, we need to underscore at the very outset that God is the One Who seals us. Being sealed by the Holy Spirit is a divine act. It is something that God does. It is God's initiative, It is God's doing. It is God's power. It is God Who seals us. In another treatment of this matter the Apostle Paul says, "Now he which stablisheth us with you in Christ, and hath anointed us, is God; Who hath also sealed us, and given the earnest of the Spirit in our hearts" (II Corinthians 1:21-22). God has sealed us! So, when we speak of being sealed with the Spirit of God, we speak of an act of God in our lives. God is the One Who initiates and enacts the sealing. God is the One Who seals. God is the One Who performs the act.

The second important fact is that the Holy Spirit is the seal. As Ephesians 1:13 says, "We are sealed with that Holy Spirit of promise." That little word "with" is in the instrument which seals believers. This underscores the doctrine of the Trinity since God the Father chooses us, God the Son redeems us, and God the Holy Spirit secures (seals) us. We are sealed with the Holy Spirit.

Commitment to Christ

Not everyone is sealed, because the sealing of the Holy Spirit is accompanied by a personal commitment to Jesus Christ. That is what he says here. "In whom ye also trusted, after that ye heard the word of truth, the gospel of your salvation..." (Ephesians 1:13). Then, when you trusted Him "ye were sealed." Every person who has received Jesus Christ as his personal Savior has been sealed with the Holy Spirit. That reception of Christ is accompanied by the sealing of the soul by God through the instrumentality of the Holy Spirit. The sealing of the

Holy Spirit is God's certification that the new believer belongs to God.

What this means is that God forces His way on none of us. No man is compelled, no man is forced against his will. Always the acts of God, the encounters with God, the experiences with God that are meaningful and lasting in our lives accompany our willingness and our commitment to Him. Being made in the image of God means we can say "No!" to God and God will abide by our decision. God does not overwhelm, overrule or overpower our lives. He abides by the willing commitment of our lives. When we hear the gospel and we trust in Christ, God seals us with the Holy Spirit.

This sealing takes place at the time of conversion. The translation, "In whom after that ye believed," is very unfortunate. The original text contains a participle which should read, "Upon believing, or having believed, or when you believed, you were sealed with that Holy Spirit of promise." It is an instantaneous act that takes place in the heart of the individual when a person gives himself to Christ.

Now, all of that may be well and good, but what does it mean to us? We need to understand exactly what takes place when a person receives Christ as Savior. We should know what we received when we believed. It is important for us to know what God offers to believers as we deal with those who have never been saved. It will help us relate to them just what God has in store for them. It will also help us to dispel doubt and to understand the depth and the breadth and the meaning of what God offers to every person through Jesus Christ.

God's Unique Possesion

The Greek word *sphragidzo* is translated "sealed" in Ephesians 1:13. It is a word used to relate that a transaction is completed. It indicates that a purchase has been made, a title deed has been transferred, or a sale has been consumated. In the process, an exchanging of ownership has been performed. That is exactly what the Apostle Paul was talking about when he said, "Know ye not that your body is the temple of the Holy Ghost which is in you, which ye have of God, and ye are not your own? For ye are bought with a price: therefore glorify God in your body, and in your spirit, which are God's" (I Corinthians 6:19-20).

In a related passage the Apostle Paul says that the sealing of the Holy Spirit "is the earnest of our inheritance until the redemption of the purchased possession" (Ephesians 1:14). To be sealed with the Spirit of God means that we belong to God. It means He has indelibly imprinted Himself in us and He owns us. He has marked us. In the Greek language the word is used to refer to a seal that identifies and marks the ownership of something. The seal sets that object apart.

Such a sealing was doubly meaningful to Christians of that day, as it would be to Jewish people. One of the customs and practices of the Hebrews priests was that when they were preparing a lamb for sacrifice, they would go to the flock and choose a lamb. After a careful, minute scrutiny of every aspect of the physical nature of that lamb to insure that it was perfect, a temple seal was placed upon the lamb. The sacrificial lamb needed to be as completely perfect as was possible. So the priests would investigate and evaluate the lamb. When the lamb had been accepted and proved to be without spot and without blemish, the temple seal would be placed upon that lamb. That seal meant that the lamb had been accepted, that it had been set apart, that it had been marked as a sacrifice. It was sealed. It now belonged to God and was going to be used to the glory of God. That seal meant that no one else could have the lamb. The Hebrews and early Christians understood this, and when Paul said, "You are sealed with the Spirit of God," they understood that it meant they were set apart and marked for God. They did not belong to themselves. They belonged to God.

The Christians at Ephesus would also understand Paul's allusion to the seal. Ephesus was a great trade city. It was a great maritime city, and one of its principal commodities was lumber. One of the customs of the trading of lumber in the great maritime city of Ephesus was that a buyer would pick out certain lumber and when he had agreed what he wanted to purchase and had purchased it, he would put his seal on it. He did not need to take the lumber with him at that time. He could leave it stacked there at the city. It would be placed there in a storage area, and it might be days or weeks before he would send a representative to claim it. This agent would come bearing his seal, and he would find the wood that had been marked with the seal of the owner. Then he would claim the wood and take it as his own. As Paul wrote, he knew that his readers would understand his allusion. It is a vivid portrayal that when we believed, we were sealed, we were stamped, we were set apart, we were marked for ownership by God. To be sealed by the Holy Spirit means that we belong to God.

Permanence of the Seal

In addition to showing that we belong to God, being sealed with the Holy Spirit is a sign of permanence. The seal itself, and the very usage of the word, reveals that something had been done that could not be changed. In the Old Testament, when Daniel was thrown in the lion's den, a seal was affixed to the door. That seal asserted that Daniel had been cast into the lion's den and nothing could change or alter his sentence. He must stay in that place unto the required time was over, and nothing could change it. When Jesus' body was placed in a tomb, the seal of the Roman Emperor was placed upon that stone and upon that sepulchre. In effect that seal said, "It is the intent of the Roman Emperor that this stone will forever be closed." Now, obviously, intending to do something and having the power to do it are two different things. The Roman Emperor did not have the power to keep that stone over the entrance to the tomb. Unlike the Roman Emperor, however, when God seals something he has both the intent and the authority or power to keep it sealed. As a result, there is a permanency involved when God seals your life with the Holy Spirit.

This sealing is the "earnest of our inheritance until the redemption of the purchased possession" (Ephesians 1:14). Paul wants his readers to know that they have been sealed, they have been set apart, they have been marked for God. His brand is upon them and it will stay there until the redemption day itself. People often talk about falling from grace, or losing their salvation. There is no way to conclude that when we understand the truth of the permanence of being sealed with the Holy Spirit. God says that when we are saved, we are sealed until the day of redemption.

What God seals, He is able to keep sealed. That is why Paul said, "Being confident of this very thing, that he which hath begun a good work in you will perform it until the day of Jesus Christ" (Philippians 1:6). That is why Peter said that Christians "are kept by the power of God through faith unto salvation ready to be revealed in the last time" (I Peter 1:5). We are sealed until that last time and in that day it will be revealed. We have been sealed by God and He will claim us as His very own. Once we have been sealed we cannot become unsealed. When God seals us, we are secure.

The sealing of the Holy Spirit is an act of God in your life. If being sealed by the Holy Spirit were something we had to do, then that sealing would be something that we could change. Since it is something God does, then only

God can change it. Since God does only what is perfect, complete and permanent, we can rest assured that this act in our lives is forever. God has sealed us. There is a permanency about it. He has sealed us until the day of redemption. As the Apostle Paul says, "Grieve not the holy Spirit of God, whereby ye are sealed unto the day of redemption" (Ephesians 4:30). God's act in our lives is perfect, complete and permanent, and there are many references in the Word of God about this very thing. To be sealed by the Holy Spirit means that we have had a permanent experience in our lives.

Down Payment of the Holy Spirit

The sealing of the Holy Spirit which occurs when we receive Jesus Christ as Savior not only indicates that we are God's permanent possession, it provides a down payment for the future inheritance that will come to every child of God. It speaks of anticipation. This sealing is a completed work which has a continuing result for each believer. Paul declares that this "is the earnest of our inheritance" (Ephesians 1:14). What is "the earnest"? It means exactly what you think it means. When I came to Dallas and purchased my house, I placed earnest money down. That earnest money did not purchase the house, but it was part of the purchase price. It was the down payment, and it secured the purchase for me. It was earnest money. It meant that someday I intended to complete the entire transaction and the house would be mine completely.

To be sealed with the Holy Spirit, who is the seal of God in our lives, is to have the earnest, the down payment of our inheritance. The seal is itself the down payment of our future inheritance in Christ. Paul continues, "until the redemption of the purchased possession, unto the praise of his glory" (Ephesians 1:14). The text should actually

read "unto the redemption of the purchased possession."
The word "until" is the same word as is translated
"unto" at the end of the verse. It is the preposition *eis*
and it means "unto" or "into." It has a goal or aim in
view. It is not concerned with time whatever. I do not
know why the King James translators translated that preposition two different ways in this passage. They are both
the same word. In Ephesians 4:30 the same term is
translated "unto," when Paul writes "unto the day of
redemption."

The Holy Spirit is the earnest of our inheritance "unto
the redemption of the purchased possession." If we say
that something is going to take place "until" sometime,
we imply that we have something that sometime in the future is going to be altered or completely different. That is
not the case with our being God's permanent possession.
If we say that we have been sealed with God's Spirit
"unto the redemption of the purchased possession," we
assert that what has happened is a part of that future
prospect. When we were saved, we were sealed by the
Spirit of God and we have a little bit of heaven in us right
now. What we will experience in the future is a fullness of
the Holy Spirit as we, the purchased possession, are
removed from this scene and are claimed by God for
Himself.

The difference between the eternity that comes into our
perfected in the final day of redemption is a difference of
degree and not of time. We have a small taste of it here,
we have the earnest of it, we have the down payment of
it. Think for a moment back to those times when your
heart was so full you thought you were going to burst
wide open and spill over on everybody around you. A
cherished friend of mine speaks about such a time as
"when God busts a honey jug in your heart." Did you
ever have that happen? God just broke a honey jug and

you were so excited you could hardly stand it. You were really blessed. God was so real to you that you loved your Christian brethren and you even loved those who hated you. There was just something sweet and wonderful in your heart. That is just a sample, just a taste. That is just a down payment. That is just the earnest money. That is just God's way of whetting our appetites. Someday, when we come to be with Him, we are going to experience it in real perfection. What a wonderful truth! The fellowship we enjoy here is just a little bit of heaven. I must confess that I am selfish. I want that little bit of heaven right now. That is what God has given us here. He is the down payment. He is the earnest of our inheritance. What we experience now is just a foretaste. It is just a sip. It is just a glimpse of the glory we will experience when God takes us home to be with Him as His purchased possession.

If you have not tasted that little bit of heaven down here, I should give you this warning. This warning is for those of you who have nights of anguish and agony and depression that settle in upon your soul. It is for those of you who are apart from God and wonder if life is really worth living. You need to understand that the bitterness and anguish and depression and despair you experience apart from God is also a down payment. It is the down payment of hell! You get just a taste of it here. You can multiply it into infinity, and that is what hell is. So, you will either experience the down payment of heaven or the down payment of hell in your life.

At conversion, when we give our hearts to Jesus we are sealed with the Holy Spirit. He forgives us of our sins. He takes away our guilt. He gives us just a little taste of heaven. When He gives us a clear conscience and a purpose for living and an abundant life, it is just a foretaste, just a sampling of what is coming over there. To be sealed by the Spirit brings the great prospect of the future.

Kept for Purity

The Apostle Paul declares, "Nevertheless the foundation of God standeth sure, having this seal, The Lord knoweth them that are his. And, Let every one that nameth the name of Christ depart from iniquity" (II Timothy 2:19). All that means is that you can depend upon the foundations of God. Write it down, stake your life upon it...you can believe it. When God says something, you can believe it is going to take place. "The foundation of God standeth sure, having this seal...." What seal? The term is the noun form of the word we found in the first chapter of Ephesians. It refers to the next statement: "The Lord knoweth them that are His." There is our possession again. That is the seal of God. We have been purchased by God, and God knows those who are His. But here is another aspect of belonging to God. "Having this seal, let everyone that nameth the name of Christ, depart from iniquity." When you have been sealed by the Spirit of God, there is the demand of purity that comes upon your soul. You cannot disregard God's law and be true to Christ. When you accept Christ as your personal Savior you are sealed by the Spirit and that sealing demands purity in your life. To be sealed by the Holy Spirit means that we are to be pure in our life dealings. We are to practice purity by departing from iniquity.

You say, "Now wait a minute. I sin every day." I know that. But the difference is not whether or not you sin. It is what you do with your sin. If you can sin and get away with it, it indicates that you have not been sealed with the Holy Spirit. When we have been sealed with the Holy Spirit, there settles down upon our souls an eternal uneasiness whenever we rebel against God. Whenever we say "No!" to God, we just cannot get away with it. So, we bring our sins back to God, not to beg His forgiveness, but to confess our sins. That is what the beloved John says: "If we confess our sins, he is faithful and just to forgive us our sins, and to cleanse us from all unrighteousness" (I John 1:9). That is what a Christian does with his sins—he confesses them to God. He yields them back up to God. He does not harbor them, he does not hang onto them. If he does, they sour in his heart. They bring despair and depression to the child of God. So, he confesses them. God says that if we confess them, He will forgive and cleanse us. He will straighten out our relationship and restore us in fellowship. To be sealed with the Spirit of God means that we will practice purity and avoid sin in our lives.

A New Position

To be sealed with the Spirit of God also means that we have a new position. The Apostle Paul put it like this: "But God, who is rich in mercy, for his great love where with he loved us, even when we were dead in sins, hath quickened us together with Christ, and hath raised us up together, and made us sit together in heavenly places in Christ Jesus (Ephesians 2:4-6). We have a new position. We now are children of God. That is what Paul meant when he said, "And because ye are sons, God hath sent forth the Spirit of his Son into your heart, crying, Abba, Father. Wherefore thou art no more a servant, but a son; and if a son, then an heir of God through Christ" (Galatians 4:6-7). He declares essentially the same truth in Romans 8:16-17. We are no longer separated from God as strangers and outsiders, we are children of God and we are heirs of God and joint-heirs with Christ. What he is saying is this, "Stand up. You have a new position. You are a child of the King. You belong to God. He is your Savior. He is your God."

One of the translations of the noun "seal" from Ephesians 1:13 is "signet ring." A signet ring represented authority. No one was given the privilege of wearing a signet ring unless he had authority to wear it. That signet ring meant that the person who had it could exercise all the authority of the one who owned the ring. It represented authority and power. Let me tell you what that means for us. We do not need to grovel in the dust at the mercy of sin, at the mercy of Satan. We need not alway be driven about and tossed about by the temptations of life, only to be disappointed in ourselves and our failings. We do not have to be because we now have a new position—we are wearing God's signet ring. We have all of the authority of God in our souls. We have the authority to pray. "Therefore (in the light of all of this transaction between God and man) let us come boldly unto the throne of grace" (Hebrews 4:16). We do not need to go begging to God. We are His sons. We can go boldly before Him and make known our requests. We have power and authority to witness. Jesus declared, "All power is given unto me in heaven and in earth" (Matthew 28:18). Later on He said, "Ye shall receive power, after that the Holy Ghost is come upon you: and ye shall be witnesses unto me..." (Acts 1:8). We do not ever witness alone. There is no such thing as going by ourselves to witness. God is always there. He is always by our side. He has given us a position of power. We have that position throughout this life. Whatever we face, we belong to God. We are His. We have a position of authority and of power. The seal of the Holy Spirit is our signet ring that shows we have God's authority and power, for He gives it to us when we accept Christ as our Savior.

Presented for God's Use

Earlier I mentioned that once a priest had selected a lamb, and certified the lamb as being without spot or blemish, he would stamp it with the temple seal. That seal indicated that the lamb was to be presented to God.

Likewise, we have received the mark of possession. There is a vast difference between us and a lamb. The lamb cannot say, "No!" We can. We ought to respect our bodies as "a living sacrifice, holy, acceptable unto God, which is your reasonable service" (Romans 12:1). This is to be done in light of all that God has done for us. When we have been sealed with the Spirit, we have been certified for service. We have been presented to God for His use, and we willingly do it out of love and appreciation for all that He has done for us. We are set apart, presented to God for His use.

Praise to God

There is one other aspect of being sealed with the Spirit that I wish to mention. The purpose of the sealing is to let us know that there is more to come. It is to let us know that there is a wonderful consummation of all things "unto the praise of his glory" (Ephesians 1:14). Do you know why people are saved? They are saved to bring glory to God. Do you know why you have been saved? To bring glory to God. You have not been saved to enjoy your salvation, though there is great delight and great joy in it. You have been saved in order to bring glory to God. In speaking of salvation, Paul asserts that it is "to the praise of the glory, who first trusted in Christ" (Ephesians 1:12). And in Philippians He declares, "being filled with the fruits of righteousness, which are by Jesus Christ, unto the glory and praise of God" (Philippians 1:11). The writer of Hebrews says, "let us offer the sacrifice of praise to God continually" (Hebrews 13:15).

The Book of the Revelation is so graphic that it is almost impossible to contain ourselves when we read, "the four and twenty elders fell down and worshipped him that liveth forever and ever" (Revelation 5:14). When we see Him, we will realize that whatever we did was all for His glory. Then we can join in with the myriads to say,

"Worthy is the Lamb that was slain to receive power, and riches, and wisdom, and strength, and honour, and glory, and blessing" (Revelation 5:12). That is why we were created. That is why we have been made new creations. Every man in Christ is a new creation for the glory and honor of God. Concerning all of the hosts of heaven, the Bible says, "and the number of them was ten thousand times ten thousand, and thousands of thousands" (Revelation 5:11). That description defies imagination. You cannot add it up upon a computer fast enough. Millions of people saying with a loud voice, in unison, "Worthy is the lamb that was slain to receive power, and riches, and wisdom, and strength, and honour, and glory, and blessing. And every creature which is in heaven, and on the earth, and under the earth, and such as are in the sea, and all that are in them, heard I saying, Blessing, and honour, and glory, and power, be unto him that sitteth upon the throne, and unto the Lamb for ever and ever" (Revelation 5:12-13). That is why we were saved—to bring glory to God.

Can you imagine how tired and disgusted God must get when we scurry about trying to get glory for ourselves? Imagine His dismay as we try to enhance our position or try to build up our reputations. All our lives are His. Everything we do is for Him. It is all for His glory! Every bit of it is for the glory of God, the honor of Christ. That is why we were sealed, set apart, and sanctified for Him. We are His and are to be used as he chooses. We have been sealed for that purpose.

That is why Paul admonished us, "And grieve not the Holy Spirit of God, whereby ye are sealed unto the day of redemption" (Ephesians 4:30). If we are not going to grieve the Spirit of God, then we are going to have to let repentance be a daily affair. We are going to have to confess our sins daily. We are going to have to lay before

Him our littleness, our critical attitudes and our bitterness. Those things that tear away at the strength of our soul will have to be confronted. We are going to have to lay them before Him. If we are not going to grieve the Spirit of God, we are going to have to obey Him—perfectly obey Him. That has real meaning for many of us. Christ is to be the Lord of our lives as well as our Savior. We need to bow our knees before Him and claim His forgiveness, His control for our lives. Only then will our lives be to the glory and honor of His Name.

CHAPTER IV

Grieving the Spirit

When we receive Christ by faith, we set our seal that God is true (John 3:33). In other words, we seal God. We declare that God is true. God is right. God is God. By reaching out to God in faith, we receive Christ. At that point we are converted and God seals us with the Holy Spirit. In the New Testament world, the seal was a brand. It was a mark of identification. It is the same in our conversion experience. It is God's way of saying, "You are my own." It is something that happens at the point of conversion. Although the sealing of the Holy Spirit has nothing to do with our behavior, we are admonished not to grieve the Holy Spirit (Ephesians 4:30). In other words, as Christians we may not always live as we should, but that has no bearing on the fact that we are sealed with the Spirit of God. Nevertheless, we are admonished to grieve not the Holy Spirit of God, by whom we are sealed unto the day of redemption (Ephesians 4:30). The thing we need to understand is that when we become saved, the Holy Spirit comes to live in us. God is a Spirit. As a spirit, God needs a body in which to live. God, through His Holy Spirit, lives in the bodies of believers. We are the temples in which God lives.

That is why Jesus said to His disciples, "Greater works than I have done, you will do" (John 14:12). How can this be so? Because Jesus was limited to one body, but when he returned to the Father He sent the Comforter, the Holy Spirit, who lives in the bodies of all believers. He now has much more freedom to move about and to do His works. Although God is looking for a body in which to live, He never forces Himself on anyone. He never forces Himself on the unbeliever to save him. Just as He never forces His way into the heart of the unbeliever to save him, the Holy Spirit never forces His way into the believer's life to sanctify him after he is saved. He seals every believer at conversion, but as far as His filling and using believers is concerned, the Holy Spirit will not force it. Man has the capacity to rebuff God and to resist Him. This is called "grieving" the Holy Spirit (Ephesians 4:30).

Although the Holy Spirit is God and God is infinite, He can still be grieved. When I say the Holy Spirit is grieved, I am not speaking of the grief someone might feel whose feelings have been hurt because he has been mistreated. That is not what Paul is speaking about when he says, "Grieve not the Holy Spirit." The grief to which Paul refers comes not because of what you have done to the Holy Spirit to hurt Him, but because you have restricted Him from doing something in you that He wants to do. That is the grief that causes great sorrow to God when we sin. It is grief to the Holy Spirit who knows how to perfect us. It is grief to the Holy Spirit who knows how to bless us, guide us and give us victory. When we shut the door to His leading and control of our lives, it grieves Him because He knows what He could have done if we had permitted it.

The grief of the Holy Spirit is similar to what I experience when people come to me for counsel. I say to them, "If you will do this, as God's Word declares, I can tell you how the outcome will be. But if you do not do it, I

can still tell you what is going to happen." Frequently individuals will leave my office and not do what I have admonished them to do. Then I am grieved. Do you know
why? I am not grieved because they have hurt me. I am
grieved because I know that it is needless pain. I know
that it is useless sorrow. I know that if they would listen to
what God had said in His Word they could avert and avoid
that pain and sorrow. If they would yield to His Spirit,
they would not have to endure such a thing. I know that,
and it grieves me to see them suffer needlessly.

Now, on a much grander scale, if you would multiply
that grief, that emotion and that compassion by infinity,
you would know something of the grief of the Holy Spirit
in the lives of God's children. It is a deep and godly grief.
It is a compassionate grief. The Holy Spirit knows the
needless pain we are going to bear because we have not
allowed Him to fill us and to direct us. That is what Paul
means when he admonishes us to "Grieve not the Holy
Spirit of God whereby ye are sealed unto the day of
redemption" (Ephesians 4:30).

In that verse we are also told that we are sealed unto
the day of redemption. What day is that? Paul is speaking
of the redemption of the body. The soul is redeemed when
we are saved. The body will be redeemed when the Lord
Jesus comes again and gives us a new body and we are
like Him. We are sealed unto that time. God the Holy
Spirit never leaves us. He is with us, but we can grieve
Him. In Ephesians 4:25 through 5:4 the Apostle Paul lists
twelve things that can cause the Holy Spirit to be grieved.
They are very practical things. They are things right down
where we live, and we need to take a look at them.

Lying

"Wherefore putting away lying, speak every man truth
with his neighbour: for we are members one of another"
(Ephesians 4:25). The first thing that grieves the Holy

Spirit is when the believer lies and misrepresents the truth. The word for "lying" is the Greek word *pseudo*. You have heard that word in many English words. *Pseudo* means "false" or "counterfeit." It asserts that something is false, misrepresented or pretended to be something other than what it is in reality. A "pseudonym" is a false name, a counterfeit name or an assumed name. By using the term *pseudo* Paul indicates that any time God's children misrepresent the truth, they grieve the Holy Spirit. Now, what are some of the ways you can misrepresent the truth?

We misrepresent it by what we say. We can misrepresent the truth by lying. We can lie about someone with the words we speak. Any time we speak something that is not absolutely the truth, we lie. The words from our lips speak wither truth or lies.

We also can lie by what we do not say. What that means is that those of us who listen to gossip are just as bad as the people who tell it. We are just as guilty. We stand just as condemned under God when we listen and do not stop it. We can be hypocritical, we can be guilty of a *pseudo,* a lie, by what we do not say.

We can be guilty of lying by our lives. If we say, "I am saved," and we live like the Devil, we are liars. God's Word says as much: "If we say that we have fellowship with him, and walk in darkness, we lie, and do not the truth... He that saith, I know him, and the truth is not in him" (I John 1:6, 2:4). We lie by what we say, by what we do not say and by how we live.

If any of these things are a part of our lives, if we have misrepresented the truth by what we have said, by what we have not said or by what we are in our lives, we have grieved the Holy Spirit. I am speaking of any misrepresentation or anything that would be considered a put-on, a counterfeit, a pretense.

"For we are members one of another" (Ephesians 4:25). When we lie we affect the whole body of Christ! We are on the same team. Do not lie about me. If you have a problem, talk to me about it. Let us share it together—we are partners on the same team...members of the same body. It grieves the Holy Spirit when the body fights against itself. Can you imagine what it would be like if every morning you had to settle a fight between your right hand and your left hand? You do not even have another hand to stop it. How could you stop it? What a frustration that would be. Imagine how it grieves the Holy Spirit when there is warring among the members of the same body. That grieves the Holy Spirit.

Anger

"Be ye angry, and sin not" (Ephesians 4:26). Let us turn that around: "do not sin in your anger." We can be angry and not sin, but when our anger turns to wrath, when our anger turns to rage, when our anger turns to bitterness, when our anger turns to grudge-carrying, we sin. It is all right for Christians to be angry, provided we do not sin while we are angry. We are exhorted not to let the sun go down on our wrath. In other words, we can be angry under the proper circumstances. Jesus was angry on several occasions. He was angry because of what He saw. He spoke out against the hypocritical religion of His day. He spoke out against the money changers in the temple. His anger was not because of their changing money in the temple, but because of their stealing from the people. Since the Mosaic Law required every Israelite to keep certain feasts in Jerusalem, and because they were scattered throughout the ancient world, they needed someone to exchange their money so they could purchase their temple sacrifices. Jesus drove the money changers out of the temple because they were cheating, not because they were changing money. He demonstrated to us how we can be angry and sin not. He was angry but He did not sin. We, too, can be angry and not sin. Any time we are angry so that it goes out of the bounds of control, or outside our spiritual involvement, we grieve the Holy Spirit. In that condition we are angry and we sin.

Giving the Devil Place in Your Life

"Neither give place to the devil" (Ephesians 4:27). Actually this statement is a part of the previous verse. It really should read like this: "Do not sin in your anger, let not the sun go down on your wrath because when you do, you give place to the devil." Let us go a step farther. Any time we give place to Satan in our lives, we grieve the Holy Spirit. Any time we allow Satan to have control in any area of our lives, to have influence in any area of our lives, we sin. When we give place to Satan in our lives, we grieve the Holy Spirit.

Dishonesty

"Let him that stole steal no more" (Ephesians 4:28). Paul here informs us that it grieves the Holy Spirit when we are dishonest, when we steal. Now, what is stealing? Stealing is taking something that is not ours. If we copy answers from somebody else's paper at school, it is stealing. It is really a problem for Christians who attend classes where most of the students do not see anything wrong with it. A survey several years ago showed that in one junior high school 95% of the students did not see anything wrong with cheating. When we copy somebody else's work, it is stealing. If we are having problems in our spiritual lives, it could be because we are cheating at school. We cannot be right with God if we are stealing.

It grieves the Holy Spirit if we take something that is not ours. When I get ready to have surgery I do not want a doctor who cheated his way through medical school to perform the operation. I want a doctor who did his homework. I want a doctor that did it himself and did not depend on somebody else to do it for him. When he gets me in that operating room, there will be no opportunity for him to rely on somebody else's work. He cannot cheat in that situation without endangering my life. The truth is that when we cheat, we cheat ourselves. We are the ones who are cheated. When we steal, we cheat ourselves. It is dishonesty. It is sin. It grieves the Holy Spirit. Every form of dishonesty grieves the Holy Spirit.

Corrupt Communication

"Let no corrupt communication proceed out of your mouth" (Ephesians 4:29). The word "communication" is the Greek word *logos*, and it means "word" or "content." "Corrupt" is the Greek word *sapros*, and it means "rotten." Paul says, "Do not let rotten words come out of your mouth." That is a most expressive way to identify what comes out of our mouths. Our language tells others about our relationship with God. Do not let rotten, worthless words come out of your mouth. Let the words that come out of your mouth be "to the use of edifying, that it may administer grace unto the hearers" (Ephesians 4:29). The test of whether or not we ought to say something is not its truthfulness. If what we say does not minister grace to the people to whom we speak we should not say it. It is rotten, worthless communication. We may know something bad about someone who is dear to others. Just because it is true does not give us the right to say it to someone. Just because it is true does not give me the right to unload on you. I will not have administered grace to you. I will have administered harshness. I have made your burden heavy. Grace means more than just unmerited favor here. It means a divine kindness administered as salve to the soul. It is undeserved, and it is beneficial to the recipient. When someone bites out at me, my human self wants to fight back. It wants to say what is true. It wants to read to him the "Riot Act." If I do that, I may be giving him what he deserves, but grace is something he does not deserve. My words need to administer grace to him even when he may not deserve it.

Divisive Spirit

"Let all bitterness, and wrath, and anger, and clamour, and evil speaking, be put away from you, with all malice" (Ephisians 4:31). This statement does not mean that we are to put these things away from us when we have malice. It means that we are to put malice away along with these other things—bitterness, wrath, anger, clamor. These are violent words. They are deeply emotional words. Look at "bitterness" for instance. If we are bitter about anything, we grieve the Holy Spirit. If I do something against you, then I am wrong, but if it makes you bitter then you are wrong. In the first instance, I grieve the Holy Spirit, in the second you grieve Him. Bitterness may aggravate the person to whom it is directed, but it will consume and destroy the one who is bitter. Every time we are bitter it becomes strife within us, and it consumes us. Bitterness grieves the Holy Spirit as it consumes us. For God's sake, we need to get bitterness out of our lives. We need to commit it to God.

The word "clamor" actually means "incoherent shouting." It portrays someone running about just babbling and crying—all torn apart. Anything that tears us apart or tears the fellowship of the body of Christ apart, grieves the Holy Spirit. That is why some of the greatest judgments of God in this life are upon good, godly people who at one time served God, but then became bitter and angry and divisive within the fellowship of the church. A Christian wrapped up in bitterness and divisiveness is living in a hell of his own making. Being torn apart, he clamors and upsets the whole body while he grieves the Holy Spirit.

"Evil speaking" is the word "blasphemy." It refers to ruining someone's reputation by saying things about him. It, too, conveys the notion of divisiveness, as does "malice." Malice is more devastating than bitterness, clamor, or even blasphemy, since it involves premeditation. It is hatred that is plotted and planned before it is concluded. It shows the end result of bitterness that is left to grow and develop. These things grieve the Holy Spirit.

Unkindness

Now the Apostle Paul turns to the other side of the coin. "And be ye kind one to another, tenderhearted, forgiving one another, even as God for Christ's sake hath forgiven you" (Ephesians 4:32). Anytime we are not kind or anytime we are not tenderhearted toward each other, we grieve the Holy Spirit. We all know what kindness is, and we need to be kind to one another. Everybody is having a hard time in this life. We do not have reason to run around passing judgment on people because we do not know what burdens they carry. We need to be kind to them. We, also, need to be tenderhearted toward them. Do you know what it means to be tenderhearted? It means that I hurt when you hurt. It means that your grief is my grief. It means that your burden is my burden. It is not only sympathy but empathy among God's children. Any time it is not true in our relationships with one another, we have grieved the Spirit. Being kind and tenderhearted is always hard in the flesh, because it is not natural for us. It is natural for us to be rough around the edges and to be abrasive to those with whom we come in contact. It is easy and natural for us to be critical and contentious. That is natural, but when the Spirit of God is in control of our lives, there is a kindness and a tenderheartedness that goes forth. As Paul indicates in Romans 5:5: "For the love of God is shed abroad in our hearts."

64

We grieve the Spirit when we are not allowing Him to spread God's love through us.

Paul goes on to say we should be "forgiving one another." "Forgiving" is a beautiful word. It is the same root as the word "grace." In essence it indicates that we are to forgive someone who does not deserve to be forgiven. It has nothing to do with the attitude of the one being forgiven toward our forgiveness. He may say, "I do not want it." Every once in awhile someone becomes very vicious and brutal. When they have offended someone else, or hurt someone who says, "I forgive you" they might say, "I do not want your forgiveness. Keep it, do not waste it on me." Whether they want it or not, they have received what they did not deserve—forgiveness. That is grace. It is unearned or unmerited favor. When forgiveness is not a part of the relationship among God's people, we have grieved the Holy Spirit. Now, you think for just a moment. Is there someone, anyone, against whom you are holding a grudge? Is there anyone you have not forgiven? Maybe your parents? Maybe your brother or your sister? Maybe your pastor or a staff member in your church? Maybe a deacon or leader in your church? Maybe a friend at school? Maybe a boy friend or a girl friend? It could be almost anyone. Is there someone you have not forgiven? Regardless of what their attitude is toward you, if you have not forgiven them, you have grieved the Holy Spirit.

Lovelessness

The next exhortation is to "walk in love, as Christ also hath loved us, and hath given himself for us an offering and a sacrifice to God for a sweetsmelling savour" (Ephesians 5:2). Anytime we do not walk in love, we grieve the Holy Spirit. If we love each other, we are going to be patient with each other. Love includes patience. If we love each other, we are going to be concerned about each other. Love includes concern. Anytime love is not characterized in our lives, we grieve the Holy Spirit. Hate and bitterness are words that do not even belong in a Christian's vocabulary as they relate to people. The Bible says we are to hate sin, but we are to love the sinner. We are to walk in love. Anytime we do not walk in love, we grieve the Holy Spirit.

Impurity or Immorality

Paul has another exhortation for us: "But fornication, and all uncleanness, or covetousness, let it not be once named among you, as becometh saints" (Ephesians 5:3). Such things are not becoming of Christians. Not only should we not practice fornication and all uncleanness, we should not even talk about them. Do not let it even be named among us. Nevertheless, anytime any kind of immorality is in our lives, we grieve the Spirit of God. And that is difficult for us to avoid. It does not really matter what it is. If it is immorality of the mind, where we lust and where we think the thoughts that lead us to actions of immorality, it grieves the Holy Spirit. If there is immorality of any kind in our lives, we grieve the Holy Spirit of God. We grieve the Spirit when we compromise at the point of morality. When we do, we need to confess it before God who will forgive us and cleanse us from it. As for immorality, do not even let it be named among you.

Foolish Talking

Then Paul adds that we should practice "neither filthiness, nor foolish talking, nor jesting, which are not convenient" (Ephesians 5:4). Foolish talking refers to inane and silly talking. If we jest, it should be in good taste, it should be "convenient." The better use of words, however, is for thanking God. "But rather giving of thanks" (Ephesians 5:4). Anytime our lives are not filled with thanksgiving to God, we grieve the Holy Spirit. The word here for "thanks" is *eucharisto*. It is the same term used by the Roman Catholic Church to refer to the Lord's Supper—the Eucharist. It is a term that speaks of giving thanks, or thanksgiving. It is thanking God for what He has done. Anytime our lives do not have thanksgiving in them, we grieve the Holy Spirit. Now, you say, "If you knew what happened to me, you would not be happy either." Paul declares, "Giving thanks always for all things unto God and the Father in the name of our Lord Jesus Christ" (Ephesians 5:20). It means exactly what it says. When there is a tragedy in our lives, thank God for it. God will turn that tragedy into blessing. God is going to make us stronger because of it. God is going to make us better because of it. We can thank God because He is actually going to do it—if we thank Him. Any time thanksgiving is not a part of our lives, we grieve the Holy Spirit. We should not just thank God for the good things, we should thank Him for everything. Thank Him for the sadness. Thank Him for the disappointments. Thank Him when things do not go as we plan. Thank Him when our hearts seem to be broken. We need to thank Him when we are depressed and disillusioned. We should thank God for all these things as well as for all his benefits.

It is thanking God for these things that enables us to gain the victory over them. We live victorious lives when we have thankfulness for whatever we experience. We can never have victory over the circumstances of life until we thank God for them. There is something about thanking God that cleanses us of a burden and takes it away. Any time we are not thankful, we grieve the Holy Spirit. Now, the Spirit of God was placed in us when we were saved. We were sealed with the Spirit. We were stamped indelibly with the print of God upon our lives by His Spirit. All of us who have been saved, have been sealed. When the sealing of the Spirit of God comes upon our lives, God the Holy Spirit comes to dwell in us. God tells us to be very careful that we do not grieve the Holy Spirit.

We are exhorted not to grieve the Spirit of God. Do not grieve Him in our minds. Do not grieve Him in our hearts. Do not grieve Him in our words. Do not grieve Him with our actions. Do not grieve the Holy Spirit. When we grieve the Holy Spirit, we interrupt our relationship with God. When we refuse to follow His will for our lives, we have interrupted and disturbed our fellowship with God. We have grieved the Holy Spirit of God. Do not do it.

God has provided for us all the way into eternity. God has given us victory, now and forever. We should not grieve Him who lives in us, who has sealed us with His own image. Paul reminds us to "grieve not the Spirit by whom ye were sealed unto the day of redemption."

CHAPTER V

Too Soon to Despair

Following his betrayal of Jesus Christ, who was arrested and delivered to Pilate, Judas had some second thoughts. He was distressed by what he had done and he tried to undo the whole thing. Judas had made a mistake. The Bible says, "Then Judas, which had betrayed him, when he saw that he was condemned, repented himself, and brought again the thirty pieces of silver to the chief priests and elders, saying, I have sinned in that I have betrayed the innocent blood. And they said, What is that to us? See thou to that. And he cast down the pieces of silver in the temple, and departed, and went and hanged himself" (Matthew 27:5).

We do not know all his motives for betraying Jesus. There is no way for us to understand all that went through his mind during the series of events. He may have been trying to force Jesus to lead a revolt against Rome. Perhaps he thought Christ would be the one who would deliver Israel from the bondage of Rome. His betrayal of Jesus may have been his way of forcing the issue. It may have been his plan for this betrayal to force Jesus to take political and military power and lead a great rebellion against Rome. There are other possibilities. He may have been a greedy, self-serving man who did what he did for the betrayal money. One thing is for sure, we will never know in this life all that went through his mind.

One thing we can know for sure, however, is that once the die was cast, Judas had second thoughts. This passage says, "And when he saw that Christ was condemned, he repented himself." The word "repent" in this verse is not the same word that we find used elsewhere in the New Testament to mean "a change of heart," "a change of direction," "a godly sorrow for sin." In the original language, it is a different word altogether. The word used here means "remorse." In fact, our text could read, "And Judas, eaten up with remorse, with despair, went out and hanged himself." He was in despair of God. He despaired of himself. As he viewed the situation, all was lost. There seemed to be no way out of his dilemma. There was no avenue of escape. There was no hope. So, he ended it all.

Although we live in the twentieth century, I believe we can sympathize with Judas. If there was ever a desperate age, it is the one in which we live. The word "desperate" simply means that we are "at the point of despair." We are at the end of our rope. We have nowhere to turn, nowhere to go. Ours is the age when over and over again, thousands of times daily, people are brought to a place where they seem to have no hope. They have no avenue of escape for the problems in their lives.

As I read this passage of Scripture, there came upon my heart a terrifying desire to jump into the setting of the New Testament in order to grab Judas, if I could, and say, "Judas, wait! Just wait three days!" I could not do that, and Judas did not wait those three days. Instead, he despaired. As a result he missed the resurrection! All he saw was Christ condemned, and because he was condemned, he knew Jesus would die. Thus, he despaired, he panicked, and he ended his life. He missed the greatest event in all of human history—the resurrection of Jesus Christ. In reality, it was too soon for him to despair.

What a tragic sin despair is. It can overtake us when we get caught in a situation, and our lives seem to take a turn we do not understand. When problems and situations crowd in upon us, we may give up, we may despair. But if we are Christians we need not despair. "Hopeless" is not a Christian word. It is not to be found in the Christian's vocabulary. Hopelessness is for the person without God, it is not for the Christian. It should not be in our hearts at all. "Hope" is what the Christian enjoys. Not only hope in the world to come, but in the world in which we live. There is no situation that should appear hopeless to us. There is no time in our lives when it is too late for us to invite God into it. There is no experience we can encounter that is beyond the means of God to come and to heal it. He can comfort and strengthen us anytime we turn to Him. We do not have to despair over any matter.

As I look about today, both inside and outside the church, I see evidence that many people have despaired because of the circumstances of their lives. Let me urge you not to despair. It is a sin to despair of God. To despair, to say there is not hope, when God says there is, is a great sin. God declares He is powerful enough to take care of our needs. He can change our defeat into victory. If we say, "No, you can't," and we despair, we push God out of the picture and call Him a liar. That is a grievous and tragic sin. When we assume that it is too late, it is too hopeless, it is too desperate to invite God into our lives, we despair too soon.

God's Provision

For some of us life has come to a tragic, screeching halt. We may have tried the best we can to make a go of it, but things have not come out right. We may have had a degree of success, and those around us may think that we have something going for us. Yet as we look into our hearts, there is a desperateness, there is despair. We do not know where to turn, where to go. We have despaired of God's Provision for our lives. Let me urge you not to despair of God's provision.

God has made provision for our salvation. The death of Jesus Christ was sufficient for the salvation of all men. He died for our sins, and not for our sins only, but for the sins of the whole world (I John 2:2). Whoever will may come and receive salvation as a result of His provision for us. There is power enough in the blood of Jesus Christ to heal our broken hearts if we will not despair of His provision and will appropriate it for ourselves. None of us are so deep in sin that we cannot have our lives resurrected by Christ. None of us are so far from God that we cannot be drawn to His heart. We have not rejected Him so many times that His love for us cannot draw us to Himself. If we do not despair of God's provision, we can receive Christ and begin our lives anew. We can begin afresh if only we do not despair of God's provision for salvation.

In addition to our salvation, God has made provision for our security. The God who saves us can also keep us. I am so glad that my salvation does not depend upon me holding onto it. My fingers are too short for that. My hands are too little for that. Even if my hands were as big as some of yours, they would not be big enough. We cannot hold onto our salvation in our own strength. Peter tells us that Christians are kept, are held, by the power of God (I Peter 1:5). God secures us. He has provided for our sins now and for all of eternity. He has provided for our security. We should not let Satan tell us we have missed something. Nor should we let Satan tell us that there is despair for us as children of God, because there is victory in Christ for each and every one of us. We are held by the power of God. Whenever a Christian sins, it is unlike the lost person who can sometimes sin and seemingly have no remorse of heart or conscience about it. As children of God we cannot sin and get away with it. In fact, when we sin, our hearts and our consciences smite us. That in itself is evidence of God in our lives. As a result, we can confess our sin and God will forgive us of it and cleanse us through His provision for our lives. Once forgiven and cleansed we are held by His power. Let us commit ourselves anew and afresh to Him and claim that provision for our lives.

When things come into your life, when the roof falls in, when life tumbles in about you, when your plans are rearranged, when things do not go as you think they ought, when they do not go as you have planned, when things are shuffled about, when there is a detour in your life, when there is an interruption in your schedule, when life collapses about you, do not despair! God says, "All things work together for good to them that love God, to them who are the called according to his purpose" (Romans 8:28). Our task is to make sure we love God. To love God means that we must repent of our sins and trust God. When we give our hearts to God, He has promised in His providence to care for us. No matter how desperate the situation might be that God has allowed to develop in our lives, we need not despair of God's providence.

If the beloved Apostle John had despaired when he was exiled, there would be no Book of the Revelation. If he had despaired when he was marooned on the Isle of Patmos, he might have said, "This is the end. I will never see my family, I will never see my friends. Life has collapsed, I will just quit." He could have sat on that forsaken isle and felt sorry for himself. Had he done that, we would have missed the beauty of the Book of the Revelation from his pen. He did not despair. He knew that God had somehow put him there. Personally, I am convinced that he had to get alone so he could not be distracted in order for God to reveal to him the glory that is portrayed in the Book of the Revelation. That kind of revelation does not come to someone on a busy street. Nor does it come to one in a crowded sanctuary. It comes in the isolation of the isle. It comes in the marooning of exile. The Apostle did not despair even when what happened to him seemed to be the worst thing that could happen. I am convinced that the church was up in arms. I am certain that those who loved John were concerned, and doubtless many people said, "Oh, God, why did you do this? Why did you let it take place?" Nevertheless, they did not despair. They prayed for John. John committed it to God. Out of his heart, touched and anointed by the Holy Spirit, came the Revelation to our hearts. His example for us is that we should not despair of the providence of God.

James said, "Count it all joy when you enter into divers temptations" (James 1:2). When something comes along to test our faith we should rejoice and count it all joy. When God commanded Abraham to sacrifice his son Isaac, it was a real test of his faith. The writer of Hebrews tells us that Abraham believed God so much that he believed that if he actually killed Isaac at the command of God, God would raise him from the dead (Hebrews 11:19). Where does faith like that arise? I will tell you where we do not get it. We do not get it from the time when everything goes right, when everything goes our way, when nothing goes wrong, when life never tumbles in, when there is never difficulty. The only way to get a faith that grabs hold of God even when there is no evidence God is there is by faith in God's providential care for us. The only way we can have a faith that believes God when there is no evidence that God is even listening is to trust in His providential care for us. The only way we can have that kind of faith is to not despair in the providences of God as they come into our lives. In the midst of every situation, we need to claim the presence and the victory of Christ in our lives.

Some of us are in the midst of the most critical days of our lives. When we are in the midst of experiences that have threatened to crush us, or which seem to push us aside and destroy us, we need not despair of the providence of God. Why? Because all things really do work together for good to those who love God and are the called according to His purpose.

God's Prophecy

History is moving toward a great climax. The Bible points to a time in the future when Christ will return to the earth. In fact, the Bible presents more information about the second advent of Christ than it does about His first advent. The Bible says more about Christ's return for His saints than it does about His birth. Because of this prophecy of the future, Christians ought not despair about their circumstances in this life.

Peter declares, "He isn't really being slow about his promised return, even though it sometimes seems that way. But he is waiting, for the good reason that he is not willing that any should perish, and he is giving more time for sinners to repent" (II Peter 3:9—*Living Bible*). In God's time, Jesus Christ will come again. The hope of the church is the return of Christ. The hope of the world is the return of Christ. That church which has been used down through history to shape the world for God has been comprised of those who did not despair of His promised return. Instead, they looked for Him to come again.

We, too, look forward to Christ's return. We look to that great climax of history, that time when Jesus Christ will return to the earth and will set up His kingdom. At that time every knee will bow and every tongue will confess that Jesus Christ is Lord! Hallelujah, He is coming! Do not give up on it. Do not despair of the projection of God about His promised return. He will accomplish that which He has promised, and He has promised to come for His own.

God's Purpose

We should not despair of the purposes of God. God has a will for our lives. He has something for us to do. I am speaking about those things that God leads us to do that seem inexplicable by man's logic. Sometimes those things do not make sense to us. We cannot understand why, but God says, "Do it!" We are left with no alternative but to do it. One thing I learned a long time ago is that we do not always have to have a reason for doing what God tells us to do. There will be times when it will not make sense. There will be times when we just cannot reason it out. No logic can wrap itself around it. No mind can comprehend it. But when God tells us to do something, and there is the confirmation that this is the will of God, we should not despair. We should do it! Sometimes our hearts grow heavy. Although we do not get tired of the work of the Lord, we get tired in the work. At times our weaknesses and the purposes of God seem to be burdensome to us. But, we should not despair of the purposes of God. Paul admonishes us, "I beseech you, brethren, by the mercies of God that you present your bodies a living sacrifice, holy acceptable unto God which is your reasonable service. And be not conformed to this world: but be ye transformed by the renewing of your mind, that ye may prove what is that good, and acceptable, and perfect, will of God" (Romans 12:1-2). God has a will for our lives.

There is much in my own life that I can identify with Paul as he came into Asia Minor to visit churches on his second missionary journey. After he had visited the churches he had established on his first journey, he desired to establish some new churches in a new area. As he looked around for the most obvious place to go, it became evident that such a place was further up in Asia Minor. As Luke records it, "Now when they had gone throughout Phrygia and the region of Galatia, and were forbidden of the Holy Ghost to preach the word in Asia, after they were come to Mysia, they assayed to go into Bithynia: but the Spirit suffered them not" (Acts 16:6-7). Everywhere Paul wanted to go, God said, "No!" Imagine the frustration! Here was an apostle living in the will of God. He was used of God to establish churches and to write a large portion of the New Testament. He was not a rebel running from God. He was doing what God wanted him to do. He did not have evil desires. He was not working for self-fulfillment or pushing his own ego. He simply wanted to tell people about Jesus. Yet, God said, "No!"

Whenever God tells us "No," it does not necessarily mean that we are out of the will of God. Paul had a sincere desire to please God. There is no evidence in this passage that he needed to repent, back up and say, "All right God, I am sorry." He simply had a desire to serve God. But God had another purpose for him. Paul thought that the greatest place he could possibly go to minister was the area of Asia. He thought that this was the place where the gospel ought to be, but God said "No!" Then, God revealed His plan. This passage says, "And they passing by Mysia came down to Troas. And a vision appeared to Paul in the night; there stood a man of Macedonia, and prayed him, saying, Come over into Macedonia, and help us. And after he had seen the vision, immediately we endeavored to go into Macedonia, assuredly gathering that the Lord had called us for to preach the gospel unto them" (Acts 16:8-10).

The interesting thing about this whole incident is that it opened Paul's ministry to new levels. His greatest contribution to Christianity was not in Asia, it was in Europe. He took the gospel to the West and it went from Europe to America and to the very place where we live. God said, "No," to the apostle Paul because He had something better for him.

What if Paul had thrown up his hands and had despaired? What if he had said, "God, it just does not make sense for me to go into Asia." What if he had said, "God, my heart is right. I want to preach and I know there are people who need to be saved there, but I want to preach here where there are even more people who need to be saved?" God said, "No!" He had a different purpose in view for Paul and the Apostle listened and obeyed God's direction for his life. We should not despair if God has shut the door upon the desire of our hearts in service for Him. We need to look upon His direction creatively. We need to look upon it providentially. We need to understand that God is getting ready to open another door for us. You see, God never closes a door without opening another. He never says "No" in one direction without saying "Yes" in another. Do not despair when God closes a door. It may be that the purpose of God that seems so distressing at a particular moment is really the greatest opportunity we will ever encounter to make an impact upon our world for God. Do not despair of the purposes of God.

God's Punishment

Do not despair the punishment of God. The writer of Hebrews says, "My son, despise not thou the chastening of the Lord, nor faint when thou art rebuked of him: For whom the Lord loveth he chasteneth, and scourgeth every son whom he receiveth" (Hebrews 12:5b-6). Sometimes God has to intervene with a judgment upon our lives to chasten us, to punish us.

I would say two things about God's punishment of believers. In the first place, none of us has a right to tell anyone else that God is punishing them. I have no right to say to you that what has happened to you is the hand of God punishing you. In addition, if we have committed ourselves to God, each one of us will know whether or not our experience is of God. We will know because the Holy Spirit bears witness with our spirits.

The most frightened person in the world ought to be the person who thinks he is saved and is not aware that God is chastening him when he sins. If we are saved, God is going to scourge us when we rebel against Him. Our scourging may be in the form of a terrible guilt of heart that drives us to our knees as it did Simon Peter when just a glance of his Savior broke his heart. The chastening rod of God smote the heart of Simon Peter and he wept bitterly. He did not despair, he repented. We should not despair. Nor should we get bitter, resentful or angry with God. If we confess our sin to Him, He will cleanse our lives and restore us to fellowship with Him.

"If we say that we have no sin," John declares, "we deceive ourselves and the truth is not in us. If we confess our sins, he is faithful and just to forgive us our sins, and to cleanse us from all unrighteousness" (I John 1: 8-9). God will make us right with Him and make us right with ourselves. He will cleanse us and forgive us. We should not despair if God has reached into our lives to chasten us. We should confess our sin to Him and make fresh our commitment to Christ. The kind of faith we must have is the kind that never varies. It is not swayed. It is single-minded and directed to Christ. James speaks of double-minded people, tossed about like a cork upon the sea, blown like children by every wind that comes along (James 1:5-8). We should not be like that. Instead, we should have a faith that hangs onto God and simply says, "I do not understand it, but I am claiming what you have as mine." We do not always have to feel that God is doing what we have asked Him to do, but we do have the right to claim it. When we claim what is ours, in His time we will feel the touch that we need in our lives.

It is persisting with God in prayer in the dry season, when it seems that He does not care at all, when there is no evidence that He hears, it is persisting at that time that makes possible the cool refreshing times when the Spirit of God is real in our hearts. We need to keep claiming what is ours.

Rivers grow crooked by dodging difficulty to follow the line of least resistence. Highways become crooked, narrow and dangerous for the traveler as they follow the contour of the land. Men become crooked the same way. We lose heart the same way. When we dodge difficulties, by despairing when it seems that life tumbles in on us, we give up and become something less than what God intends us to be. We need not despair. God is not dead. Nothing is impossible with God. Out of every situation there is hope in Jesus Christ. We need to keep looking up. As we keep looking to Him, He will either change our circumstances or change us in our circumstances. He will bring victory to bear in our lives if we do not despair of God's punishment in our lives.

Let me exhort you not to be like Judas who despaired and missed the resurrection. Jesus is alive. He is in our hearts. He is in our lives. He is in His church. He longs to reach this world for Himself. Do not despair. It is always too soon to despair because it is never too late to bring God into our difficulties. It is never too late to commit our lives to Him, for He is there.

Finally, do not despair God's presence. Claim Christ as Lord. He is here. He is ready to invade our lives, to fill our lives like a hand fills a glove. If we will claim it, if we will give ourselves in faith to Him, we will experience the glory of the resurrection all over again. As we obey Him, as we reach out in hope and in faith He comes into our lives.

Many of us may have reached the point of despair, but it is not too late. It is not too late to bring God into that situation. It is not too late to bring God into that home, into that business, into that life experience. It is always too soon for us to despair. God's provisions are more than adequate to meet our every circumstance. Do not despair.

CHAPTER VI

Worship Is Not a Spectator Sport

It is important for us to worship together because together we create an atmosphere. Now an atmosphere is intangible. We cannot see it, but we can feel it, we are aware of it. When we come to worship, we create an atmosphere of concern, an atmosphere of informality, an atmosphere of spontaneity. All these things go together to make it possible for us to meet God. That is what worship is all about. What is worship? What does it mean to worship? We have so many misconceptions about it. In our day we have the idea that just because we have been to a church building for a stated length of time, we worship. Unfortunately that may not be so. We might come to church every time the doors are open and never worship, because worship is not a spectator sport. Worship is not watching somebody perform. Worship is not simply being a sideline viewer of something that is taking place before us. Worship is something we do together.

Predominately in the Word of God, throughout the Old Testament and the New, worship involves a congregation. It involves many people gathered together in a common purpose of expressing love, respect, reverence and obedience to God. It is not possible for us to pull an order of service from the Bible, but there are certain ingredients that are seen in worship in the Bible. We know that prayer had a great place in public worship. Scripture reading was involved in the early worship, as was preaching and teaching. On a number of occasions Jesus would read a passage of Scripture then close the book and speak to the people. Instruction had its place in the worship experience, and it resulted in some response on the part of the people. We also know that worship in the New Testament was open, enthusiastic, informal, evangelistic and edifying.

The prophet Isaiah gives us five key ingredients of all true worship. "In the year that king Uzziah died I saw also the Lord sitting upon a throne, high and lifted up, and his train filled the temple. Above it stood the seraphims; each one had six wings; with twain he covered his face, and with twain he covered his feet, and with twain he did fly. And one cried unto another, and said, Holy, holy, holy, is the Lord of hosts: the whole earth is full of his glory. And the posts of the door moved at the voice of him that cried, and the house was filled with smoke. Then said I, Woe is me! for I am undone; because I am a man of unclean lips, and I dwell in the midst of a people of unclean lips: for mine eyes have seen the King, the Lord of hosts. Then flew one of the seraphims unto me, having a live coal in his hand, which he had taken with the tongs from off the altar: and he laid it upon my mouth, and said, Lo, this hath touched thy lips; and thine iniquity is taken away, and thy sin purged. Also, I heard the voice of the Lord, saying, Whom shall I send, and who will go for us? Then said I, Here am I; send me" (Isaiah 6:1-8).

In these verses we can see the ingredients of real worship. One of the great tragedies in America today is that we have little real worship and have come to take the formal worship of the church for granted. Public worship has become a very commonplace experience without any particular appeal for our lives.

Preparation

Many times people come to the service and they go away saying, "Well, I just did not get anything out of it." That may be because the first ingredient of worship is preparation. We do not casually worship God. We prepare to worship God. Our text says, "In the year that king Uzziah died I saw also the Lord." Isaiah had been to the temple many times, and doubtless he had had many experiences. But at this particular time his heart is uniquely prepared to worship. He is driven to the house of God upon the wings of sorrow. He is driven to the house of God because of the grief of his heart. He has lost one he loved and, in that grief and in that sorrow, his heart is prepared, his heart is conditioned. He is reminded again of his inability to face even the most simple relationship of life apart from God. Thus, with a prepared heart he comes to the temple to worship.

Preparation is extremely important in worship. We need to ask God to speak specifically to us and to bless us and to lead us into a new experience with Him before we go to worship. Preparation is vital to a meaningful worship experience. Earlier in Isaiah, God has asked, "To what purpose is the multitude of your sacrifices unto me? When ye come to appear before me, who hath required this at your hand, to tread my courts?" (Isaiah 1:11-12). God is asking, "Why in the world are you doing this?" That seems a strange question. God had commanded Israel to offer sacrifices. God had, in fact, demanded it. Now He asks what is its purpose. He goes on to say that He is fed up with their offerings and acts of worship. Why is God like this when He commanded His people to do it? "Bring no more vain oblations; incense is an abomination unto me; the new moons and sabbaths, the calling of assemblies, I cannot away with; it is iniquity, even the solemn meeting. Your new moons and your appointed feasts my soul hateth; they are a trouble unto me; I am weary to bear them" (Isaiah 1:13-14). That is a strange thing for God to say. Why did God say that? "And when ye spread forth your hands, I will hide mine eyes from you; yea, when ye make many prayers, I will not hear: your hands are full of blood" (Isaiah 1:15). God's attitude was based upon their lack of preparation for worship. Their hands were full of blood. They had not prepared themselves to come before Him. They were not ready to worship God. They had ritualistically gone through the motions of worship. Such behavior makes God sick to His stomach. That is what Isaiah says. His people were not prepared to come before him in worship.

The Psalmist asks, "Who shall ascend into the hill of the Lord? or who shall stand in his holy place? He that hath clean hands, and a pure heart, who hath not lifted up his soul unto vanity, nor sworn deceitfully" (Psalm 24:3-4). How do we get clean hands? We wash them. It takes discipline and it takes time. How do we get a pure heart? We get it in prayer. Who is the man who is not vain and profain? The man who has brought his heart to God. Who has not sworn deceitfully? The one who has guarded his words. This is the kind of person who can come to God. This is the one who can experience a genuine and vital worship experience. God simply says to us that we should not carelessly come into His presence. We must prepare ourselves for worship.

The word "sabbath" comes from an old Hebrew word. One of the roots of that word means "Stop doing what you are doing." That explains the problem we have with worship. We just cannot stop doing what we are doing.

How often we go to worship and all the time we are
thinking about tomorrow, about family, about business,
etc. We cannot stop doing what we are doing. That is
what it means to worship God—to stop doing what we are
doing. We need to prepare ourselves. We need to prepare
our hearts. Preparation is always a part of worhip. It
opens our hearts and our lives to God.

Praise

The first ingredient in worship is preparation. The
second is praise. The text in Isaiah describes the praises
of the seraphim to God. Such praise is always part of true
worship. When we read the Psalms, which were used in
the worship of Old Testament times, we find frequent
examples of praise. "When I remember these things, I
pour out my soul in me: for I had gone with the multitude,
I went with them to the house of God, with the voice of
joy and praise, with a multitude that kept holyday. For I
shall yet praise Him" (Psalm 42:4-5). The first psalm I
learned as a boy says, "Make a joyful noise unto the Lord,
all ye lands. Serve the Lord with gladness: come before
his presence with singing. Know ye that the Lord he is
God: it is he that hath made us, and not we ourselves; we
are his people, and the sheep of his pasture. Enter into
his gates with thanksgiving, and into his courts with
praise: be thankful unto him, and bless his name" (Psalm
100:1-4).

Jeremiah writes, "Praise the Lord of hosts: for the Lord
is good; for his mercy endureth for ever: and of them that
shall bring the sacrifice of praise into the house of the
Lord" (Jeremiah 33:11). Every worship experience includes praise. This can be seen in Psalm 150. Thirteen
times in six verses the Psalmist says, "Praise the Lord."
Praise is a part of our worship. Whenever we gather
together, we gather to praise God.

Participation

Worship is not a spectator sport. Isaiah was not a bystander in our text. Worship is not something we watch. It is something we do together. It involves participation. Participation involves liturgy. It includes singing, offerings and all those things. Many people get distressed when they hear about liturgy and ritual. Some of us feel that ritual is bad, but there must be some ritual in the worship experience. Ritual is like a telescope, someone has said. Its purpose is instrumental, not ornamental. It is something we look through, not at. The ritual of worship is something through which we look to God.

But, how do we use this instrument? First, we participate by singing. Singing is at the very heart of all worship. The entire Book of Psalms is an expression of Hebrew singing. Here is an example of such worship in song: "Rejoice in the Lord, O ye righteous: for praise is comely for the upright. Praise the Lord with harp: sing unto him with the psaltery and an instrument of ten strings. Sing unto him a new song; play skillfully with a loud noise. For the word of the Lord is right; and all his works are done in truth" (Psalm 33:1-4). Let us look at another: "O clap your hands, all ye people; shout unto God with the voice of triumph. Sing praises to God, sing praises: sing praises unto our King, sing praises. For God is the King of all the earth: sing ye praises with understanding" (Psalm 47:1, 6-7). Again, "I will praise the name of God with a song, and will magnify him with thanksgiving" (Psalm 69:30). Singing is a means of participation.

Look at what the Israelites did with their musicians. "It came even to pass, as the trumpeters and singers were as one, to make one sound to be heard in praising and thanking the Lord; and when they lifted up their voice with the trumpets and cymbals and instruments of music, and praised the Lord, saying, For he is good; for his mercy endureth for ever: that then the house was filled with a cloud, even the house of the Lord; so that the priests could not stand to minister by reason of the cloud: for the glory of the Lord had filled the house of God" (II Chronicles 5:13-14). Singing was and is an integral part of worship. The glory of God was demonstrated after such singing and praising of God. We should not merely listen to singing or playing of instruments. They are to be used together. It is important for us to participate as we sing together the praises of God.

We also participate in worship with our offerings. There always was a place for offerings in both the Old and New Testament. Paul reminds us to bring our offerings for the collection upon the first day of the week when we come to worship (I Corinthians 16:1-2). We have not worshipped at all until we have brought an offering to God. Jesus emphasized this, while underscoring the importance of a right attitude, in the Sermon on the Mount (Matthew 5:23-24).

In addition to singing and giving, we participate in worship in Bible reading. We worship in order to listen to the voice of God. We come together to hear the Word of God pinned to our hearts, to listen to what God has to say. We listen to His Word as it is read and presented to us. What God has to say is just as fresh and as relevant as life itself. When we listen to it, we are amazed at its impact on our lives.

Spontaneity

Another part of worship is our spontaneous and orderly response to God. Look at what God's Word tells us about that. "O clap your lands, all ye people; shout unto God with the voice of triumph. God is gone up with a shout, the Lord with the sound of a trumpet. For God is the King of the earth: sing ye praises with understanding" (Psalm 47:1, 5, 7). "Let the redeemed of the Lord say so" (Psalm

107:2). "And they sang together by course in praising and giving thanks unto the Lord: because he is good, for his mercy endureth for ever toward Israel. And all the people shouted with a great shout, when they praised the Lord, because the foundation of the house of the Lord was laid. But many of the priests and Levites and chief of the fathers, who were ancient men, that had seen the first house, when the foundation of this house was laid before their eyes, wept with a loud voice; and many shouted aloud for joy" (Ezra 3:11-12). The people in Ezra's day were laying the foundation for a new temple. Some of them remembered the old foundation that had been laid. They began to weep. The youth who had not been there when the old temple stood on the site began to shout. Their weeping and their shouting mingled together so that they were indistinguishable. There was spontaneous but orderly response to God.

In the New Testament, right in the middle of Paul's discussion on tongues, the Apostle said not to speak in the public worship of God. Why? Because people would not know when to say "Amen." Here are his words on the matter, "Else when thou shalt bless with the spirit, how shall he that occupieth the room of the unlearned say Amen at thy giving of thanks, seeing he understandeth not what thou sayest?" (I Corinthians 14:16). He goes on to say, "I had rather speak five words with my understanding, that by my voice I might teach others also, than ten thousand words in an unknown tongue" (I Corinthians 14:19). In addition, he speaks of the confusion that results and notes that God is not the author of confusion. He urges the Corinthians to do all things "decently and in order" (I Corinthians 14:40). Our spontaneous response to God should be ordered and appropriate. It should be uplifting and honoring to God. If it is a vital part of our worship experience, it will be just that.

I am reminded that the early Christians worshipped in the synagogue until they were forced out of it. Even though the people there did not believe like they did, these disciples worshipped God. Let us not allow somebody else in their spontaneity spoil our worship experience. But let us remember the principle of response, whether it is "Amen" or whether it is a hand-clap or whatever. If it is a spontaneous expression of love, commitment and praise of God, then do it. If it is not, do not do it. It pleases God when we worship Him with dignity, with order, with commitment and reverence. It also pleases Him when our response to Him is spontaneous.

Prayer

Prayer is a vital part of our worship experience. But that prayer is far more than the prayer that is voiced from the pulpit. It is far more than the invoking of God's blessing upon the service, or the gifts we present to God. The prayer to which I refer is the prayer of confession to God. If we are going to involve ourselves in real worship, we must get on our knees before God. We must confess our sins to God. This is the pattern for worship in the Old Testament. Such prayer was an important part of Isaiah's experience in the temple, and it is significant that it occurred in the house of God. Why? Because that place is set aside for worship. When we have drawn aside for worship, when we have drawn aside peculiarly and personally to listen to the sacred message of God, we have prepared our hearts for God to really enter into our lives. Our encounters with God may come wherever God finds us, but invariably those encounters are reinforced and continued through worship in the house of God. Whenever a man has had an experience with God in the great outdoors in the Bible, he built a shrine, altar, or a temple. He constructed a place where he could remind himself

that he had there experienced an encounter with God.
Either that, or the place itself became a shrine to the glory
of God. The house of God is important.

Like those believers in the Bible, we give our lives
building up the house of God, the buildings of God, so we
can bring people to God. Do not minimize the building of
places dedicated to the worship and service of God. The
writer of Ecclesiastes tells us something of our behavior in
the house of God: "Keep thy foot when thou goest to the
house of God, and be more ready to hear, than to give the
sacrifice of fools: for they consider not that they do evil.
Be not rash with thy mouth, and let not thine heart be
hasty to utter any thing before God: for God is in heaven,
and thou upon earth: therefore let thy words be few"
(Ecclesiastes 5:1-2). He asserts that we need to weigh
carefully the words that we speak in God's house. We
need to evaluate the words we speak in worship. He
charges us not to just come into the house of God and go
through the motions of worship. We need to be still and
listen to what God has to say to us. We need to be less
quick to speak and more prone to listen to God. We need
to open our hearts to him, and say no more than is
necessary. Our words may simply be "O God, be merciful
to me a sinner."

We come into the presence of God in worship as we
confess our sins in prayer. The Word of God speaks of a
great day when the people came together to worship God.
"And the seed of Israel separated themselves from all
strangers, and stood and confessd their sins, and the
iniquities of their fathers. And they stood up in their
place, and read in the book of the law of the Lord their
God one fourth part of the day; and another fourth part
they confessed, and worshipped the Lord their God"
(Nehemiah 9:2-3). Confession is at the very heart of
worship. We have not really worshipped until we have
confessed our sins to God. Unless we confess our sins, we

are like the Pharisee who came to the worship service next to a publican (Luke 18). The Pharisee said, "Oh, Lord, I thank you that I am not bad like this fellow over here." He was a hypocrite. He was self-righteous. The Scriptures tell us that the Lord condemned him for his attitude.

If we come into a worship experience and do not confess our sin, we are like the Pharisee, because worship always involves getting things right with God. That is the purpose of worship. It is an event that brings us to God. God cannot tolerate sin. God cannot overlook my sin. Before I can come to God, I must confess my sin. The confession of sin is that vital part of worship when we open our hearts to God. Paul said, "For I know that in me (that is, in my flesh) dwelleth no good thing" (Romans 7:18). The closer we get to God the more we need to be honest with God. As we lay our souls bare before God, we prepare our hearts. Then, when we come into a house of worship, we come believing God and trusting God and confessing every known sin to Him. We are prepared for a new experience with God. Confession of sin is an integral part of worship.

Commitment

The result of the prayer of confession is commitment. It brings us to the persuasion that we are to commit our lives to God. We have not worshiped until we have confessed our sins and committed our lives to God. We do not worship just because we come into a building and sit looking at the preacher. Even if we hear God's word it does not mean that we are understanding with the understanding of our hearts. There must be a commitment. There must be a time when we bow our knees before God and we claim what God has provided for us.

Isaiah cried out, "Woe is me! for I am undone; because I am a man of unclean lips, and I dwell in the midst of a people of unclean lips" (Isaiah 6:5). He confessed his sin to God, and he was forgiven. The seraphim touching his lips with the live coals indicates that forgiveness. Isaiah confessed his sin of the lips specifically, and his sin was forgiven specifically. Then he heard a voice say, "Whom shall I send and who will go for us?" Isaiah responded with the commitment, "Here am I; send me" (Isaiah 6:8). We are not going to hear the voice of God until we come through confession to kneel at the feet of God in worship. Then we will hear that voice, because God has a place of service for every one of us. There are no unimportant people with God. Everybody is somebody with God. God has something significant for every Christian. For every child of God there is a voice that would speak to us and say, "Whom shall I send? And who will go for us?" It may be across the street, around the corner, in the next county or the next state, on the east coast or on the west coast, or it may be abroad to some land whose language we cannot speak. When the call of commitment comes out of our worship experience, it is the voice of God. If we have confessed our sin and laid our hearts before God, we can say, "Here am I send me." Worship always climaxes in a commitment to God. It results in an open avowal and dedication of life to Him.

When commitment does not occur in worship, there is tragedy. Let me illustrate that. Luke 4 and Matthew 13 record the occasion when Jesus went home to Nazareth. He went into the synagogue and read a passage from Isaiah concerning the Messiah. He closed the book and said, "Today the Scripture is fulfilled in your lives. You are seeing it happen. I am the one Isaiah was talking about." Matthew, in recounting the story, said, "And he did not many mighty works there because of their unbelief" (Matthew 13:58). They did not believe Him. They refused to trust Him. They refused to commit their lives to Him. Because they did not take that step of commitment tragedy occurred in their lives. They missed the blessings that God had prepared for them. Their failure to commit themselves to Him resulted in anger, frustration and the failure of God to perform mighty works in their midst. I wonder how often that happens today in our houses of worship. We go to the house of God and all we hear is what someone else does, or says. Instead of seeing the angels of heaven attending the house of God, we see something we do not like, and it destroys our worship experience. When we refuse commitment, we often turn our service into criticism and hostility. Because of our lack of trust, our worship experience is aborted. When we do not respond to Jesus, hostility is the predictable result. That is why commitment is so important.

God wants to call some into salvation and into his service every time we meet for worship. It will not happen unless we let it happen. That is what commitment is. It is allowing God to do what God wants to do in our lives. Every time we come to worship, we need to commit ourselves to Jesus. We need not do it to be saved, for we need be saved only once, but every time we come into the house of God, and every time we kneel before God, we need to confess our sins and commit our lives to Him again. That is worship. It is active involvement on our part. It is not a spectator sport.

CHAPTER VII

The Unpardonable Sin

God is always interested in reaching the lives of individuals. God always moves in love as He seeks after man. The love of God, the concern of God and the grace of God comprise the most beautiful story known to man. But behind His every word, behind His every mention of grace, God provides a warning about what will happen if we spurn His love. God gives us ample warning about what will happen if we reject His love and grace to us. God will not tolerate man's rebellion. God will not tolerate man's sin. He promises that to man. Nevertheless, God also promises that, "All manner of sin and blasphemy shall be forgiven you" (Matthew 12:31). Is not that a beautiful promise? All manner of sin, all kinds of sin shall be forgiven. Such a promise provides hope for the man whose life is twisted and torn apart by sin. There is hope for the person who is drifting about in a limbo or existence without direction or purpose in life. There is hope because all manner of sin can be forgiven.

There is a point, however, beyond which God will not go. The Old Testament says that it is God's prerogative to cease striving with a man. It is God's initiative that His voice stops pleading with man (Genesis 6:3). In the New Testament the Son of God died upon the cross and God the Father decreed that every man who would ever be saved had to come to Him through the person and work of Jesus Christ. There is no other way. God said, "This is the way, you must walk in it." When Jesus Christ was nailed to the cross, He provided direct access to the heart of God. Jesus Christ became the door to God. There is now a direct way to the very presence of God and eternity. That way is Jesus Christ. There is a life which is eternal in nature which will bring you into fellowship with God throughout all of eternity. That life is called Jesus Christ. Still, this way and life were at the prerogative of God. He initiated it because of His love for man.

During His earthly ministry Jesus added another element to the matter by saying that there is a sin that drives God away from us. It is a sin that does not fit into the category of forgivable sins. It is an unpardonable sin. What is that unpardonable sin? It is not being a thief. Many of us are thieves. Many of us have stolen things. We have actually taken things which did not belong to us. Sometimes we have taken ideas and concepts from others in school. We call that cheating, but it is stealing. Many of us are thieves, but I am happy to inform you that being a thief is not the unpardonable sin. If being a thief were the unpardonable sin, Zacchaeus never would have made it, because Zacchaeus was a thief. If being a thief would keep a man from being saved, then the thief on the cross could never have been saved. He could never have heard Jesus saying to him, "Today shalt thou be with me in paradise" (Luke 23:43). He never would have heard that if being a thief was the unpardonable sin.

Immorality, as vile and vicious as it is, is not the unpardonable sin. God's Word plainly tells us how we are to act and how we are to conduct ourselves. The Bible tells us what is the right way for a man to act toward a woman and a woman toward a man. It gives us guidelines and if we abide by them, we enter into the richest and fullest possible human experience. If we violate those guidelines, we create agony and anguish and hell on earth for ourselves. We may be immoral, but being immoral is not the unpardonable sin. If that were so, David never could have made it, because David was immoral.

Being a murderer, as vicious as that is, is not the unpardonable sin. To maliciously plot and take the life of another individual is not the unpardonable sin even though there is a note of finality to such an act of violence. If that were true, David could not have made it, neither could the Apostle Paul. Both of them were involved in the taking of human life.

Drunkenness is not the unpardonable sin. It is ridiculous for a person to be a victim of drunkenness with all its heartache, distress and agony. Still drunkenness is not the unpardonable sin. If it were, Noah never would have made it. Noah got drunk after God spared him in the flood and he became a shame to his entire family. Nevertheless, God forgave him. Drunkenness is not the unpardonable sin.

Unbelief is not the unpardonable sin. I do not know how many times people say that the unpardonable sin is unbelief. No, it is not. Unbelief may be *unpardoned*, but it is *not unpardonable*. The Apostle Paul tells of the time when he was known as Saul of Tarsus and he was an unbeliever, but his unbelief was forgiven. You see, unbelief may be unpardoned and we may go to our graves without the knowledge of Jesus Christ and we will go to hell. But we will go to hell in spite of the fact that our unbelief could have been forgiven. God has provided a remedy for our unbelief. Unbelief is not the unpardonable sin.

Sin Against the Spirit

Well, just what is the unpardonable sin? It is a sin against the Spirit of God. "Wherefore I say unto you, All manner of sin and blasphemy shall be forgiven unto men: but the blasphemy against the Holy Ghost shall not be forgiven unto men. And whosoever speaketh a word against the Son of man, it shall be forgiven him: but whosoever speaketh against the Holy Ghost, it shall not be forgiven him, neither in this world, neither in the world to come" (Matthew 12:31-32). Now we must understand what the work of the Holy Spirit is in order to understand what this blasphemy against Him means. The work of the Holy Spirit in the earth is to magnify Jesus Christ. The ministry of the Holy Spirit is to guide us into the deep things of the Word of God and into the deep things of the maturing Christian life. It is the work of the Holy Spirit to apply to our lives what Jesus Christ has done on Calvary. The Holy Spirit is God's agent in saving us. He is God's agent of redemption.

Now the unpardonable sin is a sin against the Holy Spirit. In brief, succinct and practical terms that means the unpardonable sin is our constant, continual, perpetual and final rejection of Jesus Christ. In that rejection we affront and blaspheme God the Holy Spirit as He ministers to us. Every time we reject Jesus Christ, we are one step closer to hell. The unpardonable sin is not a sin that we can accidently commit. It is not a sin that we commit at just one moment. It is a studied, deliberate, and willful act against the person and work of the Holy Spirit.

Willful Sin Against Knowledge

The blasphemy of the Holy Spirit is a willful sin against what we know is the truth. The passage in Matthew twelve relates the incident of a man who was brought to Jesus. This man was blind and deaf, and he was possessed of a demon. He was brought to Jesus and Jesus healed him of all three ailments. The people were amazed and said, "Is not this the Son of David?" All through the Old Testament God has promised to send the Son of David, the New David, Jesus Christ the Messiah to Israel. The people looked for the Son of David to come. They looked for both a king and a kingdom. They had been taught what the Word of God had declared about the coming Messiah. Having been taught, and knowing this, the people said, "This is the Messiah, this is the Son of David."

But the Pharisees would not admit it, even though they had taught the people concerning this great truth. Although every one else know it, the Pharisees said, "No! It is not so. This man has done all these miracles by the devil. This man is not the Messiah. He is not the Christ. All of these things he has done because he is in league, he is in alliance, he is in partnership with the devil." Now the people knew better. The Scriptures had taught them to "Be strong, fear not: behold, your God will come with vengeance, even God with a recompence; he will come and save you. Then the eyes of the blind shall be opened, the ears of the deaf shall be unstopped. Then shall the lame man leap as an hart, and the tongue of the dumb sing: for in the wilderness shall waters break out, and streams in the desert" (Isaiah 35:4-6). They knew that when Messiah would come, the blind would be made to see, the deaf would be made to hear, the dumb would be made to speak and the lame would not only be healed, but they would run like a hart, like a deer. It was apparent. It was obvious. The Scriptures clearly taught it.

The Pharisees thoroughly studied the life of Christ. They had hounded Him. They had followed Him. They knew what Jesus Christ was doing. They also knew what the Scriptures taught. This passage clearly reveals that the Pharisees knew and understood that Jesus Christ was the

Messiah. They knew and the people knew, but the Pharisees refused to admit it. In fact, they blatently denied it.

Any time we understand that Jesus Christ is God's Son and that we need to be saved, and we say "No!" we are on dangerous ground. *Any time!* Every message that we hear, every witness that we receive, every experience that we have that helps us to understand that Jesus is God's Son, that He is alive today and that He wants to save us, every time we hear that and we say "No!" we take another step closer to hell.

The Pharisees sinned the unpardonable sin because of their willful sin against knowledge. This same sin against knowledge can be seen in the story of Moses and Pharaoh (Exodus 5-11). Ten times God told Pharaoh to do something. Finally God said, "Pharaoh, the game is over. That is enough. We are through with it. Let my people go." It frightened Pharaoh, and he let them go. Then one of his advisors came and said, "Pharaoh, you are foolish to let all our free labor go away. We are really going to have a problem. You had better go get them." Pharaoh agreed and took off after the Israelites. But God was through playing games. When Pharaoh tried to get close to the children of Israel in the day a cloud got in his way. When he tried to get near them at night, a pillar of fire blocked him. When he tried to force himself through God's provision in the Red Sea, he died along with all his army. Why? Because God meant business. "Be not deceived; God is not mocked: for whatsoever a man soweth, that shall he also reap" (Galatians 6:7).

Do not make any mistake about it. God reveals Himself to us again and again and we understand. We know that Jesus is the Messiah. We know that He is the Christ. The Holy Spirit draws us to Himself and speaks to us. God is not playing a game with us. God is saying to us, "I love you, I care for you, I will forgive you all manner of sin except willful rejection when you know better." That is the essence of the sin of blasphemy against the Holy Spirit—the unpardonable sin.

The writer of Hebrews warns us to be very careful lest we be hardened through the deceitfulness of sin (Hebrews 3:13). Right now our hearts may be sensitive. Right now there may be an emptiness or a gnawing in our souls. Right now there may be an awareness that something is wrong. But every time we say "No," sin deceives us. Without our realizing it, our hearts get hardened and hardened, until we cannot respond to the prompting of God the Holy Spirit.

Some of us may say, "I am living in hell right now. My life is in the grip of such things as you would not believe." It does not matter. God is not playing games with us. God wants to save us. He wants to free us. He wants to give us life. He wants to give us purpose. He wants to give us meaning. He will do it. He is not kidding with us. He is not playing games with us. He will free us from drugs. He will free us from immorality. He will free us from dishonesty. He will free us from any chain that binds our souls when we come to Him. He wants to do it. He informs us that He cares and that He has provided a remedy for all our sin and for all our ills. The unpardonable sin is our willful rejection of that knowledge. It is our refusal to take heed to the prompting of the Holy Spirit as He works in our lives.

Willful Sin Against Conviction

The unpardonable sin is a willful sin against conviction. Conviction is the task of the Holy Spirit and our willful rejection of His work in our lives is sin of great magnitude. The Holy Spirit brings conviction to our lives. The Holy Spirit creates an awareness of a need in our hearts. The Holy Spirit of God is the real presence of God in our day-to-day experience. Jesus said, "I will pray the

Father, and he shall give you another Comforter" (John 14:16). The Greek word "another" as used in this text means "another of the same kind." The Holy Spirit is the same essence as Jesus. He is just like Jesus. His task is to convict us of sin. His task is to make us aware of our need and of sin in our lives. Jesus said, "No man can come to me, except the Father which hath sent me draw him" (John 6:44). The Father uses the Holy Spirit to draw men to Christ. We cannot be saved unless the Holy Spirit draws us to God. If He did not convict us, there would be no desire for salvation in our lives. God is sovereign, and salvation is His sovereign work.

Many of us have the idea we can get saved whenever we are ready. Not so. We get saved when God gets ready. We get saved when the Spirit of God draws us to Himself. The Bible says, "Today, if ye will hear his voice, harden not your hearts" (Hebrews 3:7-8). In another place it says, "Seek ye the Lord while he may be found, call ye upon him while he is near" (Isaiah 55:6). The clear implication is this, if we try to play games with God there will come a time when He will not respond to our cry. We are going to be drawn to Christ or we will not come at all. It is the Holy Spirit who convicts and draws us to God.

Now this kind of experience happened to these Pharisees in our text. They knew that the work of Jesus was the work of God, and they had no excuse. They also knew they were to be judged by His work, as Jesus Himself said, "For judgment I am come into this world, that they which see not might see; and that they which see might be made blind. And some of the Pharisees which were with him heard these words, and said unto him, Are we blind also? Jesus said unto them, If ye were blind, ye should have no sin: but now ye say, We see; therefore your sin remaineth" (John 9:39-41). The Pharisees had come to Jesus in a personal confrontation, a personal encounter. Some of the Pharisees heard these words and asked, "Are we blind also?" Jesus responded, "If you were blind, you would not be guilty of such a terrible blasphemy as the blasphemy against the Holy Spirit of God. But you know, you have been convicted by the Holy Spirit, you know that it is true and now your sin remains forever." Theirs was a willful sin against conviction.

If the Spirit of God is dealing with us and there is a need and we know that something needs to be done, we dare not turn Him down. The unpardonable sin is a continuous, constant, perpetual and final rejection of the ministry of the Holy Spirit in our lives as He directs us to Jesus Christ. Now, who is to say when the final time is come? Who is to say when that moment will come when we will have said "No" to God for the last time? The unpardonable sin is a sin against knowledge and it is a sin against conviction. It is a sin people commit who really know better. I do not think any of us can plead ignorance of the convicting work of the Holy Spirit of God. We have heard the gospel. There are numerous radio stations that preach the gospel throughout the week. We know the gospel. We have heard the story of Christ. If asked about it, we would all respond, "Yes, Jesus is the Son of God. I believe that." Now, be very careful, because the unpardonable sin is the sin against knowledge and against conviction. What grave danger we face if we are moved of the Holy Spirit to commit our lives to God and do not do it.

The unpardonable sin is a sin beyond which God cannot go. God cannot forgive the sin after it has been committed. There is no reprieve. There is no instant replay. There is no rerun. Once the unpardonable sin has been committed, the door of grace is closed. After that, it matters not how many church services are attended. It does not matter how loudly we may cry or how earnestly we may pray. When we commit the unpardonable sin, God says, "That is it!" At that point God stops dealing with us. Our choice has been eternally made.

How do we know we have not committed the unpardonable sin? How do we know that we still have hope of being saved? Let me answer it with a question. How do you feel? If God is dealing with you, if there is a sensitive part in your heart, then you have not committed the unpardonable sin. Suppose you break your leg and go to the doctor and the doctor looks at your leg and he pokes at it. He says, "Does that hurt?" If you say, "No, I cannot feel a thing," the doctor's reply will be, "That is bad." The loss of feeling in the leg means that something has happened to those nerves and healing cannot take place. There is not sensitivity. It is dead. Now suppose that when he begins to poke on the leg the pain is severe. The doctor will say, "That is good." Pain means there is still life and healing can take place.

It is the same way in our spiritual life. We may know Christ to be the Son of God, and we may know that Jesus Christ died for us, and that we are sinners who have need of God. Still, if there is no stirring of the Spirit of God in our hearts, if there is no feeling when we hear the gospel, we may have already committed the unpardonable sin. But if there is a hunger, if there is a desire for something more than we have, if there is a longing and a yearning for purpose and for meaning, we have not yet found, God is still working with us. We should cherish that desire. We should water it with our tears. Why? Because that feeling is our sign that the Holy Spirit is dealing with us. If there is a longing, a reaching out for something, it is the Spirit of God telling us that He loves us. He is telling us that the death of Christ upon the cross can be made effective in our lives.

Now I want to ask another question. How do we know we are not going to commit the unpardonable sin now? The only one who can be sure is the person who is saved, because the Christian never commits it. No Christian ever commits the unpardonable sin. In fact, no Christian can commit it because God the Holy Spirit lives with the Christian's heart. If we have already given our lives to Jesus Christ we cannot commit the unpardonable sin. Only unbelievers can commit that sin.

Well, what about you? I do not care what church you attend. I do not care how good you may be. I do not care how kind you may have tried to be through your life. I do not care how hard you have tried or how honest you are. If you do not know Jesus Christ as your Savior, there is only one way to make sure you are not going to commit the unpardonable sin. That is to repent and turn your life over to Jesus Christ. Turn your all over to Him. He is the only way we have to God. He wants you to bring your sin, your emptiness, and your lack of direction in life to Him. He wants you to give your sin to Him so He can get rid of it.

You cannot do it yourself. You have tried to get rid of it, you have tried to get rid of that nature that is always rebelling. You have tried, but you cannot. Jesus can do it. He knows where to put your sin. He puts it in the sea of the grace of God, the sea of God's forgetfulness. He treats your sin as if it had never happened. He heals your sinful spirit. He wants to do it for you now. All you have to do is be willing. It can never happen unless you are willing. For, you see, the unpardonable sin is a willful sin and being saved is a willful act. You must make the choice of your heart and mind. You have to be willing for God to come into your life. You have to be willing to turn your life over to Jesus. There must be a commitment, a choice. It is up to you.

CHAPTER VIII

The Sin unto Death

The Bible tells us there are two great sins against the Holy Spirit. Both of them bring dire consequences to the person who commits them. The Bible calls one the "unpardonable sin." It is a sin committed by unbelievers. The other is called the "sin unto death." It is committed by Christians, as may be seen in the statement, "If any man see his brother sin a sin which is not unto death, he shall ask, and he shall give him life for them that sin not unto death. There is a sin unto death..." (I John 5:16). The Apostle John is writing about Christians praying for each other. He tells us that we ought to pray for each other in intercessory prayer.

The beloved Apostle continues, "There is a sin unto death: I do not say that he shall pray for it" (I John 5:16). In these words, John sets before us the tremendous truth of the sin unto death. His message is directed to Christians, for the entire epistle of I John was written to Christians. Look at this statement for instance: "These things I have written unto you that believe on the name of the Son of God that you may know that you have eternal life" (I John 5:13). Then, just a few verses later, John writes, "If a man see his brother...." So, when we speak about the sin unto death, we are speaking about something committed by Christians. An unsaved person does not commit the sin unto death. His sin is the unpardonable sin, which concerns rejection of the work of God the Holy Spirit in his life.

Let us return now to the matter of the sin unto death. Many people who have claimed the name of Christ have slipped into flagrant sin without any apparent punishment. I have often wondered, how some people can claim to know Christ and deny Him by their witness and their example. Although they may cling to a personal faith in Christ, everything they demonstrate to the world indicates that they live a lie. How does God put up with it? This has always perplexed me as I have wondered why God has permitted it to continue. Through study of the Word of God, I believe God has given me the answer to this matter in the doctrine of the sin unto death.

There are one or two consequences that may follow Christians who commit the sin unto death. In the first place they may be stricken with death as they commit it or shortly thereafter. A believer may sin against the Holy Spirit and sin against God in such a way that his life is taken. He may, physically, be killed as a result of his sin. There is a second consequence that may follow when a Christian commits the sin unto death. If God does not take the life, the consequences of that sin will stay with the individual as long as he lives. He will live in the shadow of that sin. He will live in the defeat of that sin. He will bear the scars of that sin.

This point is illustrated for us in the prophecy of Amos. In speaking of the plagues God sent upon Israel, Amos adds, "Yet have ye not returned unto me, saith the Lord" (Amos 4:8). Then he refers to pestilence and natural disasters, and concludes, "Yet have ye not returned unto me, saith the Lord" (Amos 4:9). He asserts that God had sent military powers to overthrow and to conquer Israel, "Yet have ye not returned unto me, saith the Lord" (Amos 4:11). This tragic statement is repeated five times in the space of six verses. In effect He says, "You have not returned to me even though you knew better, even though you were enlightened, even though you had the call of God and you meant to repent, you did not return unto me." Then Amos pronounces the judgment of God upon Israel, "Therefore thus will I do unto thee, O Israel: and because I will do this unto thee, prepare to meet thy God, O Israel" (Amos 4:12). Here is a judgment upon the people of God. It is God's promise that He will not wink at sin.

One of these days we are going to see the greatest visitation of the judgment of God upon people this world has ever seen, unless real revival comes. God will not tolerate sin. God is not going to permit people to make a mockery of Him. God is not going to allow churches to become empty with formalism and without heart and without evangelistic zeal and fervor, without bringing judgment upon them. He will not ignore Christians as they wallow in sin. There will be a judgment of the sin persistently committed by believers. It may be expressed by the death of the Christian himself.

Sin of Presumption

There is a difference between falling into sin and living in sin, between error and willful sin. The sin unto death is a sin of presumption. It is a presumptuous, willful, deliberate sin. It is not like walking along the edge of a platform and suddenly falling off the edge. The sin unto death is something that comes from an act that is planned, premeditated and brooded over. It is a sin that is carefully and willfully executed. No one forces us to do it. It comes about because there is a lust in our hearts that draws us into it. We plan to do it. We carry it out and deliberately, maliciously sin against God. It is not something that happens suddenly, although it may be judged even while it is being committed.

The Bible says, "If we sin wilfully after that we have received the knowledge of the truth, there remaineth no more sacrifice for sins" (Hebrews 10:26). God is telling us that if we willfully and deliberately sin against the Word of God and the truth of God, there is no more sacrifice for sin. Jesus is not going to come back and die for us again. He has already done that. Such sin must be judged by God. If we willfully sin and deliberately plan this sin against God's Word and Spirit, we commit the sin unto death.

David understood the sin unto death because he had committed it. David willfully and with premeditation planned sins in his life that greatly affected both his own family and the nation of Israel. He speaks about this in the Psalms. He says, "Cleanse thou me from secret faults" (Psalm 19:12). He is praying for forgiveness and he says in effect, "Cleanse me from those things that happen when I come into a situation and in the emotion and experience of that moment I sin. It is a fault that I did not anticipate, I did not plan: Forgive me of that." Now notice what he says, "Keep back thy servant also from presumptuous sins; let them not have dominion over me: then shall I be upright, and I shall be innocent from the great transgression" (Psalm 19:13). If these presumptuous sins do not have dominion over him, he will be "upright and innocent from the great transgression." He speaks as a child of God and as a priest of his people. Not only was he the king and political leader of Israel, he was their religious leader. Now what do you suppose is that great transgression? The great transgression to which David refers is the sin unto death.

Second Samuel twelve gives the background to this statement and that passage will help us to understand it.

In that instance in the life of David, Nathan the prophet
came to bring the message of God to David. Nathan did
not mention the sin of adultery, nor did he even speak of
the time David saw Bathsheba and committed adultery
with her. He did not mention this because that sin was not
premeditated. David did not willfully plan it out over a
period of time. The Bible simply says that he chanced to
look and there she was. She was fair to look upon. He sent
a servant and, in the emotion, in the attractiveness, in the
lust of that moment, he sinned.

Nathan did not mention the sin of adultery, but he did
say, "Thou hast killed Uriah the Hittite with the sword,
and hast taken his wife to be thy wife, and hast slain him
with the sword of the children of Ammon" (II Samuel
12:9). Now there is a two-fold sin presented here. David
willfully killed Uriah—he plotted it, he planned it. It was
premediatated. He knew it was against the will of God. He
knew the precepts of God and yet there came into his
mind a plan to scheme to get something he wanted in the
flesh. So he plotted and planned for it. With malicious
premeditation he killed Uriah. Then, with the same
planning and cunning he endeavored to cover up that sin
by marrying Bathsheba. He committed a second premeditated sin in order to cover up the first.

God's judgment was very harsh upon David. Look at the
words of judgment, "Now therefore the sword shall never
depart from thine house; because thou hast despised
me...behold, I will raise up evil against thee out of thine
own house..." (II Samuel 12:10-11). At this point David
comes face to face with his sin. God's judgment was pronounced. It was certain, and David understood that the
penalty for his sin was death. There was no other
provision for his willful sin.

If you read the Old Testament carefully you will find
that God never did make a provision for willful sin. He

never did! There is no sacrifice in the Old Testament for a person who deliberately plotted and planned to sin. There was no sacrifice. The penalty was always death. Always when a person sinned against the truth of God and the knowledge of God and with careful planning carried out the sin of his heart, the penalty was death. David knew this. In his prayer of confession that came as a result of God's pronounced judgment, he cried, "For thou desirest not sacrifice; else would I give it: thou delightest not in burnt offering. The sacrifices of God are a broken spirit: a broken and a contrite heart, O God, thou wilt not despise" (Psalm 51:16-17). He knew there was no sacrifice for willful sin. There is no burnt offering to cover a man's life when he willfully and with premeditation sinned against God. That is the sin unto death.

What is it God desires? He seeks confession of sin as David indicated in His prayer of confession, "The sacrifices of God are a broken spirit: a broken and a contrite heart, O God, thou wilt not despise." Commuting the death sentence for the Christian who commits the sin unto death comes only by repentance. When we willfully and with premeditation sin against God, He asks us to come to Him in repentance. God always honors that. Do not think the picture is bleak with no hope. Do not think the person who has committed the sin unto death is convicted without any recourse. If that heart reaches out to God, if that heart cries out for God, if that heart repents and claims forgiveness, God always responds. God always forgives. The sad thing is that the Christian who has presumptuously, willfully and deliberately sinned against God, generally does not care to repent. Then the judgment of God falls upon him. Then he has committed the sin unto death and the judgment of God is set.

Now be very sure that you understand that the salvation God offers you is a complete salvation. He offers you salvation and forgiveness of past sins, presents sins and future sins. The death of Jesus Christ upon the Cross cleanses you from all sins. "By the which will we are sanctified through the offering of the body of Jesus Christ once for all. For by one offering he hath perfected forever them that are sanctified" (Hebrews 10:10, 14). However, when we as Christians sin, we have to deal with the consequences of sin. God will not lessen His requirement and His judgment upon sin even in the life of a Christian.

There are some who say, "when you get saved you stop sinning." That is just not true. I know better from my own experience. I know I am saved, and I also know the kind of person I am in the flesh. I know that I have not stopped sinning. I know that except for the grace of God, the mercy of God and the access I have to the throne of God through Jesus Christ, I would be a desperate person. The Apostle John says, "My little children, I write this unto you that you sin not" (I John 2:1). But He knows that Christians will fall into acts of sin even after they are saved. As a result he continues, "But if any man sin, we have an advocate with the Father, Jesus Christ the righteous" (I John 2:1). In the preceding chapter he says, "If we confess our sins, he is faithful and just to forgive us our sins, and to cleanse us from all unrighteousness" (I John 1:9). We need to be very sure that we understand that Christians have access to God and to the forgiveness of God. God is always ready to cleanse the repentant heart.

There are, however, certain lines of conduct that bring down judgment upon the believer in a very strict and severe fashion. Look at this, for example, "Know ye not that ye are the temple of God, and that the Spirit of God dwelleth in you? If any man defile the temple of God, him shall God destroy; for the temple of God is holy, which temple ye are" (I Corinthians 3:16-17). We cannot sin and get away with it. God is going to bring us to judgment for our sins. If we live in willful sin God is going to bring down severe judgment upon us—even in this life.

Let us look at another example. The Apostle Paul writes, "For I verily, as absent in body, but present in the spirit have judged already, as though I were present, concerning him that hath so done this deed, in the name of our Lord Jesus Christ, when ye are gathered together, and my spirit, with the power of our Lord Jesus Christ, to deliver such an one unto Satan for the *destruction of the flesh,* that the spirit may be saved in the day of the Lord Jesus" (I Corinthians 5:3-5, italics added). The "day of the Lord Jesus" refers to the return of the Lord. In order for the soul of a sinning Christian to be saved for that day, Paul calls for the destruction of his flesh. In another passage Paul adds further information about this same man. He writes, "Sufficient to such a man is this punishment, which was inflicted of many. So...ye ought rather to forgive him, and comfort him, lest perhaps such a one should be swallowed up with overmuch sorrow" (II Corinthians 2:6-7). Apparently the man had repented. Apparently the man had turned from his sin and cried out for cleansing. As a result, God speaks to the Corinthian church through Paul and charges them to receive him back into the fellowship. Doubtless this man bore the stigma, the scar of his sin. There had been some punishment inflicted upon him and he continued to bear the shame, the disgrace, the consequences of his sin. He bore the punishment of his sin to his death, but God commuted the death sentence. God said, "You will not die, but you will bear the punishment and the penalty to the very end. You will bear the scars of this sin of presumption throughout your lifetime."

Now let us return to the story of David and Nathan. The Scriptures say, "And David said unto Nathan, I have sinned against the Lord. And Nathan said unto David, The Lord also hath put away thy sin; *thou shalt not die*" (II Samuel 12:13, italics added). David knew he stood under the condemnation of death. There was no sacrifice for willful, premeditated sin. So Nathan said, "Howbeit, because by this deed thou hast given great occasion to the enemies of the Lord to blaspheme, the child also that is born unto thee shall surely die" (II Samuel 12:14). The child died because of David's sin. The tragic scar that David had to bear as long as he lived was the fact that he could never forget why there was a little tombstone in his family cemetery. Nor could he forget the other elements of judgment pronounced upon him and his family for his sin. "Now therefore the sword shall never depart from thine house. ... Behold, I will raise up evil against thee out of thine own house..." (II Samuel 12:10-11). David bore to his death the consequences of his sin in his family. Absalom, his favorite son, was typical of all the children of David. Absalom rebelled against his father. He stole the hearts of the people and fostered revolution against his own father. David bore it to his death. His children disgraced him and dishonored him because of his sin unto death. As long as he lived, he could never forget the tragic consequences of his sin. His was a sin of presumption.

Sin Against Knowledge

The sin unto death is a sin against knowledge. It is important to understand that I am not referring merely to falling into sin. I am not speaking of the occasional and casual sins we commit in the course of a day. The sin unto death is a willful, deliberate and premeditated act. In addition to that, the Bible says it is a sin against knowledge. It is a sin committed by people who know better. It is a sin committed by people who know the Word of God. It is a sin committed by people who have heard God's message and know they should not do it. Because of their rebellion, they sin against the knowledge they have.

In his first epistle to the church at Corinth the Apostle Paul speaks about the Lord's Supper. In that dicussion he says, "Let a man examine himself, and so let him eat of that bread, and drink of that cup. For he that eateth and drinketh unworthily, eateth and drinketh damnation to himself..." (I Corinthians 11:28-29). Do not be mistaken about that term "unworthily." It does not mean we should say, "I am not worthy." "Unworthily" is an adverb that modifies the verbs "eat" and "drink." It speaks of the manner in which we partake of the Lord's Supper and not our personal merit. It does not address whether or not we deserve to partake of the Lord's Supper. It is concerned that we be very sure that we have turned our lives over to the Lord before we partake of the Lord's Supper. We are to be very sure that we have laid our lives alongside the Word of God. If we have not, then we should not eat. The reason, Paul says, is that "he that eateth and drinketh unworthily, eateth and drinketh damnation to himself, not discerning the Lord's body" (I Corinthians 11:29). Now notice Paul's conclusion to this matter. "For this cause many are weak and sickly among you, and many sleep" (I Corinthians 11:30). Some Christians thought the Lord's Supper to be a gay old time, a wonderful banquet. They simply enjoyed it without facing their sins and without worship from their hearts. They did not truly face God, and many of them became weak and sickly. What I am saying is this. Many of us become physically weak because we sin against God and against the knowledge He provides us about how we are to live for Him. Not all sickness is the result of sin, but "... and many sleep." Their death came because of their rebellion and sin against knowledge, their sin unto death. They have gone against God's instruction, so theirs is a sin against knowledge.

When Israel came toward the promised land, spies were sent into the land. When they returned, the majority of them said, "We cannot do it." God had already told them to go into the land. They had the command and the promise of God. They had all the history of the deliverance of God. They knew they were supposed to go into the land, but they refused to do so. Only two of the spies said "Yes." God declared that every one of the Israelites of age but those two would die in the wilderness (Numbers 14:37). This was the judgment of God. The Israelites knew the plain teaching of God. Nevertheless, even with their better understanding and their better knowledge, they sinned. As a result of their willful sin unto death, they condemned themselves to die in the wilderness.

In the fifth chapter of Acts the familiar story of Ananias and Sapphira appears. In that church, where the worship service lasted up to three hours, some of the people were hungry and some of them were needy. As a result, various Christians had been selling their possessions, pooling their resources and making sure everybody had enough to eat. Nobody was commanded to sell his possessions because there is not command in the early church for them to do it. It was a spontaneous thing. It was done out of a willing heart as a spontaneous expression of love. It demonstrated the moving of the Spirit of God in the midst of the church at Jerusalem. Now Ananias and Sapphira doubtless had seen others come with their gifts and so they thought, "We must do something." No one commanded them to sell their property. In fact, they did not want to sell all their possessions. It was not required that they sell any or all of what they possessed. They could have sold part of it and brought it to the disciples and said that they had more that they would keep themselves. They could have done whatever they desired. As time passed, they sold a part of their possessions. Then Ananias came to church and made his offering. Simon Peter asked, "What is this?" Ananias answered, "I have sold my property." Then Peter asked, "Oh, really? How much did you get for it?" "Well," said Ananias, "this is it." Peter retorted, "Ananias, why have you lied unto the Spirit of God? You knew better. You had the knowledge, but you lied." Ananias dropped dead and they carried him out and buried him.

Three hours later Sapphira appeared. She knew nothing about what had happened to Ananias. She gave the same testimony. She knew better, but she lied. There was no command of God for her to lie to the Holy Spirit. It was a willful, premeditated sin against the knowledge of God. Simon Peter said, "The feet of those who buried your husband are here for you," and she dropped dead. It would be a fearful time in our churches if God were to visit us like that! I wonder how many of us have lied to God. We did not have to do it. No one held a gun to our heads. No one said, "You have to do this." But we have lied to God. We have pretended to God. We have willfully and with premeditation told Him lies. Perhaps it was when we made a false commitment of service to Him. At any rate, I wonder how many of us have lied to God by willful, premeditated sin against His Word.

As I thought about this truth, my mind has gone back to all the problems I have ever faced in the ministry. I have thought of all the people I have had the privilege of serving as pastor. I have thought about all the people who became angry, or left in spirit or otherwise became obstinate. Yet they have said, "I am saved." They have torn down the church of God while professing to be Christians. I have thought how many of those people bear the pain of hell in their bodies until they die, because of their willful sin after that we have received the knowledge of the truth, there remaineth no more sacrifice for sins, but a certain fearful looking for of judgment and fiery indignation, which shall devour the adversaries" (Hebrews

10:26-27). God declares there is no more sacrifice for sin when we willfully sin. God is not going to send Christ to die for us again. Associated with that truth is that taught to us by the Apostle Paul when he says, "Every man's work shall be made manifest: for the day shall declare it, because it shall be revealed by fire; and the fire shall try every man's work of what sort it is. If any man's work abide which he hath built thereupon, he shall receive a reward. If any man's work shall be burned, he shall suffer loss: but he himself shall be saved; yet so as by fire" (I Corinthians 3:13-15). When the sin unto death has been committed, there remains nothing for the Christian but the Judgment Seat of Christ.

Our notion that the Judgment Seat of Christ is going to be like a great Christmas tree with the Lord sitting in the role of a Santa Claus is all wrong. We envision him calling out our names and passing out gifts for us to unwrap. I do not find that to be the description of the Judgment Seat of Christ. That is going to be a fearful time, for there He is going to burn away the dross of our lives. He is going to reveal to us exactly what we are for all eternity. If our works have been wood, hay and stubble, they will go up in smoke and we will be saved just by the skin of our teeth. We will be saved as if by fire, and some of us will discover that we committed the sin unto death in our lifetime. Someone may well ask, "When does a sin become the sin unto death?" I do not know. But this I do know. The only way to keep a sin from becoming the sin unto death is to confess it to God immediately when the Holy Spirit convicts us about it. I need to get it confessed as soon as I am aware of it. Why? Because I do not know when a sin becomes the sin unto death. I know that the sin unto death is a presumptuous, willful, deliberate sin against the knowledge of the truth God has made known to me. I also know how to confess my sin and to have it forgiven according to the will of God. The Apostle Paul tells us that we are to judge ourselves. He writes, "For if we would judge ourselves, we should not be judged. But when we are judged, we are chastened of the Lord, that we should not be condemned with the world" (I Corinthians 11:31-32). If we face our sin, if we repent of our sins, then we judge our own sin. We confess it to God, we repent of it, and God forgives it. But if we refuse, then God will judge us and He will chasten us so that we will not be judged with the world and be condemned.

What God tells us is simply that He is not going to tolerate sin in His people. If there were ever an age when God's people have sinned, it is the age in which we live. More than sixty-five percent of the population of this country claims to be Christian. Yet only a fragment of that number are actively worshipping and serving the Lord. Still fewer live according to the Spirit of Christ in the world. The fearful judgment of God is a judgment upon individuals. It spills over from them into society. The Bible says that God will visit the sin of the parents upon the children, grandchildren and the great-grandchildren. He will visit sin to the third and fourth generations. It is a simple and compelling truth that God will not and cannot tolerate sin. When sin is punished, we may bring punishment and wrath upon those who are not even connected with our sin. Our hope is to immediately confess our sins to Jesus Christ. To claim His forgiveness and to be cleansed by Him is the only way to avoid the sin unto death.

This startling truth of the sin unto death is for a very specific purpose. It is not given for me to evaluate the lives of other people and pass judgment upon their sin. It is given for me to examine my own life and cause me to honestly face myself in the Presence of my Lord. May this truth draw us ever closer to Him and cause us to stand in His power and forgiveness each day.

CHAPTER IX

When God's Patience Runs Out

There is a biblical truth stated in reverse when God says, "My Spirit shall not always strive with man" (Genesis 6:3). The truth is that God's Spirit seeks after man. God pursues us to bring us to Himself. God cares about every one of us. God is concerned for us. God loves us. God cares about what happens to us. God cares whether or not we are happy. God wants to give us life. God seeks us even when we reject Him. But as our verse states, God's Spirit will not always and indefinitely pursue us.

Adam and Eve turned their backs upon God when they disobeyed Him. They hid from Him, and He went looking for them. As He sought them, God called out, "Where are you?" One of the most exciting and glorious truths of the Word of God is that ever since that time God has personally and individually sought men in the world. What an exciting truth that is. In spite of our rejection of Him, and regardless of how bad we are, God seeks us. God loves us, God cares about us. God seeks us to offer to us His redemptive grace and forgiveness. That is a wonderful truth.

Nevertheless, the Bible also clearly teaches us that there comes a time when God loses His patience so to speak. There does come a time when God says, "I have had enough. I have given you all the opportunities that you will need to respond to my grace." There does come a time when God says, "I am through. I will seek you no more. I will pursue you no more." The Bible says, "Wherefore God also gave them up to uncleanness through the lusts of their own hearts, to dishonour their own bodies between themselves: For this cause God gave them up unto vile affections: for even their women did change the natural use into that which is against nature: And even as they did not like to retain God in their knowledge, God gave them over to a reprobate mind, to do those things which are not convenient" (Romans 1:24, 26, 28).

In describing the result of the wickedness of men in these verses, God's attitude and judgment are presented. Because of rebellion and the persistent refusal of man to do what God wants, God gave up on them and left them to their own devices. God gave them over to a reprobate mind. I do not think God ever stops caring, but there comes a time when God no longer seeks to rescue men from their sure judgment. God's patience does indeed come to an end. God's patience can be exhausted. God can give up on us.

Before He does, however, God reveals Himself to us. God speaks to us. The Bible says, "Wisdom crieth without; she uttereth her voice in the streets: she crieth in the chief place of concourse, in the openings of the gates: in the city she uttereth her words" (Proverbs 1:20). The word for "wisdom" here is a word which represents the personification of God. What the writer of Proverbs has done under the leadership of the Holy Spirit is to personify one of the attributes, perfections, of God. That personified attribute is God's omniscience, His wisdom. What he actually says is, "God, who is all wisdom, is crying in the streets, in the chief places in the city." God has sought and is seeking for man to the point where He turns him over to his own devices. Let us look at how God seeks man in this world.

God Speaks

Through the years, God has spoken to man as He has sought him. God speaks words of compassion, words of concern and words that fill the heart. God has spoken to us in the Bible. In it He tells us where He speaks. He speaks in the gates of the city, where people gather as they carry on their business activities. God does not hide His speech from us. He speaks to us in easily accessible places. We have no excuse. We live in a land where God's truth is seen on every hand. God's Word is readily accessible today. We can hear it with just a turn of the radio dial. We can hear it preached in hundreds of churches within a few miles of our homes. God's Word is readily accessible to us today.

In addition to the proclaimed word about God, He is seen in nature. The Bible says, "The invisible things of him from the creation of the world are clearly seen" (Romans 1:20). God has not hidden His communication to man. God has spoken so that we can understand. The reason God has revealed Himself so clearly is so that all men will stand before Him without excuse. We cannot say that we do not understand. We cannot say that we do not know what God is trying to say to us. The tragedy is that we know all too well what God is trying to say to us. We have not been willing to act upon what He has said. His words are accessible to us. God comes to us where we are. He comes to us to speak to us and to compel us to make a response to Him.

There is that beautiful statement tucked away in the story of the Good Samaritan which illustrates this point. The narrative relates that the man from Samaria came by, looked at the man, and that he "went to him" (Luke

10:34). That Samaritan did not do like the priest and the Levite had done before him. They backed away and walked around the injured traveler. They did not want to get involved. The Samaritan came to where he was and cared for his needs. That is what God does for us. God comes where we are and meets our needs. That is why Jesus came. Jesus was God's attempt to come to assist us in our need. He was God's way of speaking plainly and clearly to man. No longer can anyone say, "I do not understand God, I do not know what God is like." God, in His compassion has demonstrated His love and concern for us. God tells us, "If you have seen Jesus, you have seen me." He speaks where it is readily accessible and understandable to us.

What does God speak? When God speaks, He speaks words of warning. He urges "Turn you at my reproof" (Proverbs 1:23). A reproof is a rebuke. It is a warning. We had best pay attention when God speaks, because God speaks words of eternal value and importance to our lives. We can miss what we say to one another and we will not miss much. But if we miss what God says, we will spend eternity in separation from God. We will miss heaven and gain hell if we miss what God says to us. God issues words of warning from the past. We never seem to learn anything from history. The same experiences seem to come over and over again in the experience of man. Man never seems to learn from the past. That is why God warns us.

God warned the wicked of coming judgment in Noah's day. For one hundred twenty years, he warned them through Noah's preaching. Noah undoubtedly became the laughing-stock of his day. He may even have become the chief tourist attraction as he spent his time preaching and building the ark in those days before the flood. How ridiculous he must have looked as he built that ark as long as a football field. All the time he was building it he was speaking for God and was warning the people that a day of judgment was coming. He warned that a flood was to come upon the earth, but they would not listen to him. God warned them, but they failed to heed His warning.

Before God brought judgment on Sodom and Gomorrah, He sent messengers to those cities to warn them (Genesis 19:1-22). Only three people survived the event as all others failed to heed God's warning. When God speaks, He speaks so man can hear and respond. God speaks to warn man of impending judgment. In those warnings God is serious, because His judgment brings death, and death is real. God is busy speaking to our hearts, warning us that if we do not make proper preparation, we will die in our sins. By responding to God's love we receive life. Life is given to us as a gift from heaven to prepare for eternity.

Later on in history, God warned Ninevah of coming judgment. He sent a reluctant and rebellious Jonah to preach, "Yet forty days, and Ninevah shall be overthrown" (Jonah 3:4). That pagan nation repented and God withheld His judgment. He had warned them, and they responded in repentance. As a result, God extended His mercy and His grace to them.

Why does God speak? He speaks to us because He loves us. There is no other reason. I cannot understand why God speaks. I only know that He warns me of sin and of judgment. I do not know why He cares how I act or what I do, but He does. He tells me that He loves me and that He loves you. He has protected us through the years. He has shielded us from physical harm and from incidents that might take our lives in order to bring us to this point of commitment. He has brought us to the present because He loves us. He cares for us. That is why He speaks to us and warns us about sin and death.

God Acts

The Bible tells us that after God speaks and man refuses to respond, then God acts. He goes into action and moves in judgment. God declares, "I also will laugh at your calamity; I will mock when your fear cometh; when your fear cometh as desolation, and your destruction cometh as a whirlwind; when distress and anguish cometh upon you. Then shall they call upon me, but I will not answer; they shall seek me early, but they shall not find me: for that they hated knowledge, and did not choose the fear of the Lord: they would none of my counsel: they despised all my reproof. Therefore shall they eat of the fruit of their own way, and be filled with their own devices" (Proverbs 1:26-31).

Men who are judged for their failure to respond to God have dealt their own destruction, and they are going to experience it. God moves in judgment in our lives, God may indeed be the agent of that judgment, but we will have brought the judgment upon ourselves. We will have brought it upon ourselves because God has warned us, spoken to us, revealed His heart to us, pled with us and convicted us of sin. When we say, "No," to God, or when we say, "I will not listen to God," then God acts in judgment.

Surely God's patience will run out one day. It happened in Noah's day, although there was one hundred twenty years of grace and warning. Finally, God shut the door to the ark and judgment struck. Then He opened the windows of heaven, and brought such a flood that it covered the entire earth. He commanded rain for forty days and nights, and broke up the fountains of the deep. Noah and the others who were with him remained in the ark for three hundred seventy days. That is just a little over a year. It took that long for the water to subside to the point where it was safe for them to get out on top of Mt. Ararat. God warned men. He gave them one hundred twenty years of grace, and then He acted in judgment. He said, "You have brought it upon yourself. I have warned you, I have begged you, I have pled with you. You have refused to accept my message to you, so judgment will surely come."

The inhabitants of Sodom and Gomorrah were also warned. Following their warning, destruction came (Genesis 19:23-27). Throughout the prophecy of Jeremiah God warns His people that judgment is coming upon the nation. God enlisted the service of a pagan king, Nebuchadnezzar (Jeremiah 43:10) to chastise His people. God warns and then He acts. Do not think for a minute that God could not use Russia, China, or somebody else to chastise America. God used this pagan monarch of ancient Babylon to bring judgment. God did not act, however, until He had first given a time of grace and warning.

A similar thing happened in Egypt. God said to Pharaoh, "Let my people go." Pharaoh was warned, but failed to heed it. Then God brought the plagues upon Egypt as He had warned that He would do. Pharaoh did not believe God or respond to the warnings. Pharaoh did not think God would carry out His judgment on the first-born in every household. Pharaoh did not believe God, but God had spoken and He always keeps His word. He had warned Pharaoh, and then He acted in judgment.

Modern Application

We need to be very personal about all this and apply it to our own experiences. There are two ways it applies to us. There are two things that can happen when God reaches the limit of His patience. First, we might commit the unpardonable sin. This is not something that we accidentally commit. It is not a casual sin. It is a deliberate and willful sin. It is a sin against knowledge. It is committed when we know that God's Spirit is dealing with us and we say, "No," to God. When we know we need

God and we are fully aware of our need for repentance and faith, and we laugh at God and push Him out of our lives, we are in danger of commiting the unpardonable sin. It happens as an act of judgment when we continually reject God's warnings and fail to respond to Him even when we know better. At some particular point God says, "All right. This is the last time. Never again." Then we have committed the unpardonable sin. It is a sin against knowledge. It cannot be accidentally committed. On a day when Jesus was talking to the people, He said, "For judgment I am come into this world, that they which see not might see; and that they which see might be made blind. And some of the Pharisees which were with him heard these words, and said unto him, Are we blind also? Jesus said unto them, If ye were blind, ye should have not sin: but now ye say, We see; therefore your sin remaineth" (John 9:39-41). In effect Jesus said to them, "If you were blind, you would not be guilty, but since you see clearly and understand that I am the Son of God, you are guilty." The unpardonable sin is not a casual thing, it is not an unconscious thing. It is a conscious rebellion against God, a conscious rejection of Jesus Christ. It happens when God's patience reaches its limit with man. As the Bible says, "He that being often reproved hardeneth his neck, shall suddenly be destroyed, and that without remedy" (Proverbs 29:1). Sudden destruction could come as the judgment of God upon any life that rejects the Gospel. God's patience could reach the limit with a given act of rejection. When that happens, judgment comes in all its fury.

Secondly, God can also lose patience with a Christian who persists in sin. God can say to a child of His, "I've had enough of the way you are living." The Bible calls this "the sin unto death" (I John 5:16). The sin unto death occurs when a child of God becomes so reprobate and rebellious that he rejects the presence and the person of God in his life. In effect God says, "I cannot have a person who professes my name living like that before an ungodly world. My patience has reached its limit and my judgment is sure." Then God may actually take the life of the rebellious Christian. That is why Paul exhorts Christians to prepare themselves for the Lord's Supper. He says, "But let a man examine himself, and so let him eat of that bread, and drink of that cup. For he that eateth and drinketh unworthily, eateth and drinketh damnation to himself, not discerning the Lord's body. For this cause many are weak and sickly among you, and many sleep" (I Corinthians 11:28-30). The reference to "sleep" is a reference to physical death. Some have died because of their rebellious spirits against God. Every man ought to repent of his sin and be right with God when he partakes of the Lord's Supper. If he does not, he eats and drinks condemnation unto himself. God has a judgment designed for His children who desecrate His things and who rebel against Him. His patience has limitations even for His own children.

Nevertheless, God's patience with His own people is longsuffering. I am amazed at how patient God is, but He chooses to limit His patience when His children do not live under His direction and care. The Lord Jesus tells us that we are to abide in Him because He is the vine and we are the branches. When we fail to abide in Him, He says we are to be corrected. He says, "Every branch in me that beareth not fruit he taketh away" (John 15:2). He purges those of us who do not abide in Him. He destroys our physical life when we fail to live in Him. He is speaking about His people and not unbelievers. He refers to Christians who rebelled against, resisted and rejected God's Word. When they go on in their sin, God's patience does run out. God's patience reaches its limit because God loves us and cares for us. He does not want us to go on and ruin our own lives as well as the lives of others. Even His judgment is gracious.

If every one of us got what we deserved we would not stand a chance of pleasing God or attaining life eternal in Him. We would have nothing whatsoever to offer to Him. But God loves us and cares for us. He speaks to us, searches for us, reaches out to us because He wants to save us. After He saves us, He keeps reaching out and calling to us. Oh, how much God cares. But there can come a time when His patience wears out because of our sin. He does not play games with us. He gives us opportunity to prove where our trust lies. It is time for us to prove where our faith lies. When God speaks to us, we need to say, "Lord, I will not test your patience. I will not go any further. I will trust you. I will live for you. I will repent of my sins. I will turn my life over to Jesus Christ. Come and be the ruler and center of my life."

CHAPTER X

The World,
the Flesh and the Devil

If we love the world, we are going to lose what we love, The world is temporary. It will not last forever. When it dies, we lose it forever. If we love the world, we are going to be disillusioned. If we love the world, we are going to be disappointed. Why? Because the world is temporary. It is passing away. Our lust for the world also passes away. Since this is taking place, we are destined to discouragement and defeat because what we love is temporary and fleeting. It is passing away. It is dying. Do not love the world, because it is passing away. "Love not the world, neither the things that are in the world. If any man love the world, the love of the Father is not in him. For all that is in the world, the lust of the flesh, and the lust of the eyes, and the pride of life, is not of the Father, but is of the world. And the world passeth away, and the lust thereof: but he that doeth the will of God abideth for ever" (I John 2:15-17).

The way to outlast the world is to do the will of God. The world is passing away, "but he that doeth the will of God abides forever." If we want permanence, we must do the will of God. God is eternal, and the only way for us to

have permanence is to do His will. If we have given
ourselves to the world, we have set our affections poorly,
for the world is temporary. It is fleeting. It is always
passing. It is like the dewdrop. A dewdrop is just as beautiful as a diamond. The difference is that a dewdrop does
not last as long as a diamond. Compared with God, even a
diamond is fleeting and passing. It is going to be gone, it
is going to fade away. If we want permanence, if we want
to really have life and happiness, then we need to know
God and do His will.

The Apostle Paul gives us the clue as to how sin came
into the world. "For as by one man sin entered into the
world, and death by sin; and so death passed upon all
men, for that all have sinned" (Romans 5:12). Adam was
like a doorkeeper. Satan knocked on the door, Adam
opened it, and sin came into the world. When sin came in,
death walked in by its side. Both sin and death have been
here ever since. Sin entered through Adam. That is how
sin came into the human experience. The thing that we
need to be very much aware of is that sin entered when
the environment was absolutely right. Nothing needed to
be changed. Adam lived in an absolute utopia. There was
no need to change anything. Sin came into the world in
the midst of an ideal setting, in the midst of an ideal
environment. This teaches us that sin is not socially
derived. It does not come from society. Circumstances
never create sin. Circumstances may make sin more or
less active, easier or more difficult to commit, but
circumstances never create sin. We can do whatever we
wish to in this world. We can improve society until it is
absolutely perfect, and we will not have eliminated the
real problem, which is sin. Conditions may change, but sin
stays. Sin comes from man himself. Sin entered into the
human experience through Adam. Often people tell me,
"You do not understand the circumstances." We should
never use circumstances as an excuse for sin. It does not

matter what our circumstances are. Our sin does not arise from our circumstances. We are sinners. We have been sinning. There is sin in our hearts. When the circumstances are right, we sin, but the sin was already there. Circumstances never create sin. They may condition sin, but they do not create it.

The World

This world was a beautiful place when sin entered into it. In fact, we still see glimpses of that beauty when we look at the marvels of our world. God created it absolutely perfect. Then God created man just exactly as he wanted him to be. Some people say, "I just do not understand why God created me the way He did." God did not create each of us. God only created two people, and He was absolutely delighted with them. They were beautiful, intelligent and strong. They were ideal. Then sin entered and distorted God's creation and passed its curse upon all subsequent generations. Sin ruined all of God's creation, sin marred and distorted it all. A curse was pronounced because of Adam's sin. The Bible says, "Cursed is the ground for your sake; in sorrow shalt thou eat of it all the days of thy life" (Genesis 3:17). Thus a cosmic curse was passed upon this world. The beautiful creation of God now abides under a specific curse due to man's sin. When we look at the world, the first thing we can say about it is that sin ruined it.

The second thing we can say about it is that man polluted it. I am not just speaking of ecology, but that would be a good place to begin. Man has polluted the air and the waters of the earth. But there is an even worse pollution that man has committed. He has polluted the world with sin. Sin cursed man and his environment. Sin brought havoc in nature. Sin ruined it. Just as there has been a cosmic curse, there has also been a cosmic cure or redemption. "The creation itself also shall be delivered from the bondage of corruption into the glorious liberty of the children of God" (Romans 8:21). There is going to be a cosmic redemption just like there is going to be a personal redemption. This old world is awaiting the return of Jesus Christ just as we are. Why? Because at that time this world is going to be redeemed. This world is going to experience release from the curse that has been caused by man and his sin.

Sin ruined the world, man polluted the world, but let me add quickly that God loves the world. God cares about this world and everything in it. He cares about the world itself, the physical universe and he cares about man in this world. He gives enough sunlight and water for the plants to grow. He gives a wonderful balance as He appoints the seasons. God loves the world. When we read John 3:16 we do not observe the amount of love that God extended to the world, but we see the kind of love, the quality of love, with which God loves this world. He did not just sit somewhere and write stories or poems or songs about it. He showed how much He loved the world by sending His son to die on the cross. Jesus died on the cross as a testimony of the love of God for this world. His death on the cross was the means whereby God could lift the curse of sin from the world.

In addition to His love for the world, God loves us. His love has been made personal through Jesus Christ. The Bible tells us that people everywhere can see the work of God. Every man is without excuse because everyone has had enough light to know that there is a God who has an interest and concern for him. But, Jesus Christ came to personalize the love of God. He came to show that God loves you individually and specifically. God loves you and is interested in you as an individual, as a person, through Jesus Christ. The world has been ruined by sin. It has been polluted by man, but God still loves the world and man. He still cares and He still wants to reach through the fog of moral pollution and the rebellion of our hearts and love us personally. Based upon the Word of God, I can tell you that God loves us intensely and God loves us eternally, but we will never understand what the love of God really means until we love God in return. Why? Because then His love is spread abroad in our hearts by the Holy Spirit (Romans 5:5). When we commit our lives to God, we enter into the experience of His love to us. When we do, we can begin to understand the love of God.

Those who have not really tasted of salvation stand outside the love of God as it is directed to them personally. It may be that they charge that, 'God does not care for He is a god of anger and wrath who hurts and harms and damns eternally.'' But once we commit ourselves to Him and we receive the love He has given to us, we will learn that man goes to hell of his own choosing. Men live in agony and anguish on this earth because of their rejection of God's love. God loves us so much that He has provided a way for us to receive His love. If we refuse His provision, we will go to hell, literally over the dead body of Jesus Christ. Every day, in every way God is trying to give to us of His love and life. He is trying to lead us to Himself because He loves us.

The Flesh

Every one of us is a sinner. Not a one of us is free from the corruption of sin. Our flesh is corrupt. Galations teaches us about the fruit of the Spirit. It also speaks of the lust of the flesh. In that discussion, the Apostle Paul lists representative works which are derived from flesh. He writes, "Now the works of the flesh are manifest, which are these; adultery, fornication, uncleanness, lasciviousness, idolatry, witchcraft, hatred, variance, emulations, wrath, strife, seditions, heresies, envyings, murders, drunkenness, revelings, and such like: of the which I tell you before, as I have also told you in time past, that they which do such things shall not inherit the kingdom of God" (Galatians 5:19-21). These are the works of the flesh. If we seek to know what our flesh is capable of producing, we can see it in this list. In our flesh, we will never produce anything else. The very best things we can produce in ourselves is listed here.

"But the fruit of the Spirit is love, joy, peace, longsuffering, gentleness, goodness, faith, meekness, temperance: against such there is no law. And they that are Christ's have crucified the flesh with the affections and lusts" (Galatians 5:22-24). We may say, "I have two or three of those characteristics, but not all of them." But the fact is that we either have them all or we do not have any of them. The term "fruit" is singular in the text, whereas the "works" is plural. We may have four or five of the works of the flesh evidenced in us, but the fruit of the Spirit is singular, and we either have all or we do not have any. There is no indication that we can have just part of it. As we go through our life experiences, we are constantly making value judgments. These value judgments are governed by the flesh or by the spirit. There is no other option. We may think that we are doing pretty well in one area and not so well in another, but unless we daily commit ourselves to the will of God and to His purpose, we cannot demonstrate the fruit of the spirit in our lives. If we do not commit ourselves to the will of God daily, we will be governed by the flesh, and all we will be able to produce will be the works of the flesh.

If we serve the flesh, we will always reap corruption. That is what the flesh always produces. Many of our physical, emotional and other problems come because we have acted in the flesh. There is no way we can please God by operating in the realm of the flesh. The Apostle Paul asserts, "For I know that in me (that is in my flesh,) dwelleth no good thing: for to will is present with me; but how to perform that which is good I find not" (Romans

7:18). My flesh is weak. My flesh is corrupt, and its works reap corruption.

In addition, the flesh is condemned. The Apostle Paul indicates that because of Adam all of us die physically, in the flesh (I Corinthians 15:22). That is why we have cemeteries. People die because the flesh is condemned to death. That is also why we must experience the resurrection of the body when the Lord returns. When the Lord Jesus Christ comes back and we meet Him in the air, He is going to change this old flesh. We will go into eternity with a different kind of flesh. We cannot have the same flesh. So, whether we are resurrected or raptured, this flesh is going to be transformed. Why? Because the flesh is condemned.

The entire sixth chapter of Romans is written to show us that there is freedom from the flesh when it is nailed to the cross through Jesus Christ. "Knowing this, that our old man is crucified with him, that the body of sin might be destroyed, that henceforth we should not serve sin. For he that is dead is freed from sin" (Romans 6:6-7). When we open our hearts to Jesus Christ, He takes us back to calvary and nails our old selves to that cross. When that is done, we die to the penalty of sin. Yet, we die in order to live. Just as a kernel of wheat must first die before it becomes new grain, our flesh must die before it lives. We deal with our flesh and its corruption by committing it to Jesus Christ. Unless we commit it to Him, our flesh is always flesh. We can change it or remodel it, but it is still the flesh. It is still corrupt. It is still condemned. Jesus Christ can transform us. He can change it all. He can give to us a new heart. He can give to us a new life. He can do this because He has condemned sin in the flesh.

Remember what God told Moses. He said, "I have written my laws on tables of stone." As He delivered the law to Moses, it was in graven stone. Later He said, "I will put my laws into their mind, and write them in their hearts" (Hebrews 8:10). If we will permit it, we can commit to Jesus Christ our flesh and its deeds. When we do, He will crucify it with Him and give to us new life. That is the only way we will ever be liberated from our flesh, its corruption and its condemnation.

The Devil

The name "Satan" means "one who hinders or opposes." In a few words that tells us what he desires to do to us. He wants to spoil everything that is good in our lives. He tells us that God does not care about us. He tells us that the church is full of hypocrites. He tells us that we cannot live the Christian life. He begins to zero in on certain areas and tells us that we will never be any different than we are now. He wants us to get used to the way we are and to settle for nothing better in the future. He begins to lie to us. He deceives us and hinders us. He stands in our path to obstruct us every step of the way that God would lead. He is a hinderer, an opposer. He does not want us to be happy. He does not want us to have life, or to enjoy it when we have it. He wants to destroy us and everything about us. So, every step we take toward and with God is a step we take over Satan. He does not give to us what he promises. He always cheats us. He was a liar and a deceiver from the beginning. The Lord Jesus called the devil the "father of liars" (John 8:44). When he is turned loose in the last days, he will even deceive the nations (Revelation 20:8). That is his objective. The devil is a deceiver. That is all he ever has done, and it is all he ever will do. He uses deception as a device to destroy men and to divert them from God.

When Satan entered the garden of Eden, he deceived Eve. He lied to her by telling her something less than the whole truth. In effect he said, "The tree of the knowledge of God and evil is a good looking tree. God knows that if you eat of that tree, you will be as smart as He is. He does not want you to be as smart as He is, so He has given you an empty threat about death if you eat of that tree. He wants to keep you ignorant. He does not want you to have that kind of wisdom.'' When Eve saw how beautiful the tree and its fruit was, she felt it would satisfy her hunger and make her wise. She ate of it. Now part of what the devil had said was true. Indeed, Eve did know right from wrong after she ate the fruit. She understood what it meant to be separated from God. The devil had deceived her into thinking that she would be like God.

After their fall, the only way Adam and Eve were like God was in their being able to see their sin. The rest of it they did not have. They had no power. They had no peace. They only know that they were sinners. God knew that would be the result and gave them warning about it. Nevertheless, the knowledge of their sin of disobedience was the thing Adam and Eve learned. The devil had deceived them. He lied to them. He used the things of the flesh, the material things of life such as appetites, desires, and aspirations, to entice them into sin. So it is with us today. When our souls sin, our spirits descend into utter darkness and die. We are dead in sin and helpless in it until we respond to the grace of God.

When a child has reached the age of understanding and accountability and for the first time comes face to face with temptation, then Satan tests that child. He will lure and entice and attract that child into sin by disclosing partial truths and by accusing others of their shortcomings. His objective is to get that child to deliberately and maliciously disobey the will of God and the purpose of God. When the child chooses what is wrong, and deliberately goes against God, the soul sins and the spirit dies. That is when the child becomes dead in trespasses and sin by actual choice and participation. If one does not know Jesus Christ as personal Savior, he is already dead in sin. His spirit is dead, and it is going to remain dead through all eternity unless something happens in his heart to give him the new birth of life in Christ Jesus.

The devil always starts from the outside and works inward. He uses our bodies to undermine our souls. He will use them as tools to get us to sin. If he cannot use our bodies, he will use our minds. He uses our bodies and our minds as the means to get to his objective, our will. When he gets to our will, he destroys us by getting us to deliberately choose to go against God's will and purpose for our lives. God does just the opposite. God works outward from the inside of our being. God begins in our soul. He takes us apart and begins to work in our heart. He changes our heart, and our heart works on our will and our will works on our mind, which in turn works on our body. God, working from within, causes us to exercise our will over our body to do His will.

That is how we can tell if it is God or Satan dealing with us. Satan always works from the outside. God always works from within. If we want to know if it is God or Satan dealing with us, we should examine how the dealing is directed. If the dealing appeals to our flesh it is from Satan. If the dealing appeals to our heart, it is God who is working on us.

Satan's desire for us is plain. He wants to take us to hell with him. He knows that he is destined to be there for all eternity. The Bible says that Satan is going to be taken and he is going to be cast into the lake of fire forever (Revelation 20:10). He knows where he is headed, and he wants to take as many people as he can to that abode. He has a design that misery loves company, and we all recognize the fact that there is consolation in numbers. If I am miserable, it just helps me if you are miserable with me. Satan is going to spend eternity in misery and isolation from God, and he is going to take everybody with him that he can. He will deceive you. He will lie to you. He will hurt you. He will lead to destruction and death in eternal separation from God.

Knowing what the Bible says about Satan's destiny, let me tell you a wonderful thing. We do not have to wait until Satan is bound and cast into the lake of fire for all eternity to have victory over him. Jesus Christ has already defeated Satan on the cross. The verdict is in and the sentence has been pronounced. There is no question about the outcome. The battle has already been fought. The victory has already been won. When Jesus died on the cross and came up out of the grave, he showed Satan's defeat. In the meantime, Christians can experience victory over Satan now. God does not want us to be defeated or abused by Satan. He has provided the power of Jesus to help us overcome our adversary. God's Word declares, "There hath no temptation taken you, but such as is common to man, but God is faithful who will not suffer you (He will not allow you) to be tempted more than you are able; but will with the temptation make a way of escape, that you may be able to bear it" (I Corinthians 10:13). God has provided for us right now. We do not have to be pushed around or bullied by Satan. We can let Jesus deal with him for us. We are told to, "Resist the devil and he will flee from you" (James 4:7). We have power over Satan if Jesus is in our hearts. Satan cannot face up to Jesus. Everytime the devil knocks, we should send Jesus to answer the door. That is what we need to do in order to have victory over Satan right now.

Let us take a look at our enemies. They are the world, the flesh, and the devil. We live in the world that has been ruined by sin and polluted by fallen man. But God still loves us in that setting. God still cares for us. He cares so much that He wants to redeem every person living in this world. One day when He comes again He is going to redeem the very creation itself.

Another enemy is our flesh. The flesh is corrupt and it will always be corrupt. It can produce no good thing. It moves toward corruption and as a result it is condemned to die. Jesus came to triumph over the power of the flesh. "For what the law could not do, in that it was weak through the flesh, God sending his own Son in the likeness of sinful flesh, and for sin, condemned sin in the flesh" (Romans 8:3). Jesus will nail the desires of the flesh to the cross with Him. He will give to us release from the domination of the flesh.

Our third enemy is the devil, Satan. He will always act the same as he lies to us, deceives us, opposes us and obstructs us. He will try to destroy us in every conceiveable way—at home, at work, at church, at play. Wherever we are, Satan will oppose, hinder and thwart us! But he is destined to destruction. He is already defeated. We can claim our victory in advance through Jesus Christ. In Christ, "We are more than conquerors" (Romans 8:37). That means that Satan is already defeated, and we can claim our victory right now.

If we have trouble in the world, or problems with the flesh, or if Satan is giving us trouble, we can come to Jesus Christ for victory. We can let Jesus Christ handle the problems that we cannot solve. We need to have Him do what we cannot. He will be everything we so desperately need if we will but turn to Him.

CHAPTER XI

Death

Many people have a difficult time listening to preaching. We all react in different ways. Sometimes we just busy ourselves doing something else. Sometimes we just ignore the preacher, even though our eyes may be wide open and we may look attentive. Looking attentive does not mean that we are hearing anything. There is, however, a preacher to whom everybody listens. Everyone hangs breathlessly on his every word. We want to know what he says. We want to know what he has in mind. This most arresting, most sobering, most convincing, most persuasive of all preachers is death. When death speaks, we listen. We are not too busy when death speaks. We listen. Nothing is too important when death calls. There is nothing so important that it causes us to turn aside from listening when death speaks.

No matter what our age, when death speaks, we listen. The reason is, we all have a stake in what he says. We are not just talking about old people when we talk about death. Again this morning I was amazed to see how much there is about death in the newspaper. A seventeen-year-old high school student was murdered this past week. Her escort was shot in the head. The youngest United States Senator in America committed suicide. Today's paper related the story of Stacy, a beautiful child born with a disease that will cause her to wither and die. Two major kidnapping incidents have held the nation in rapt attention recently. When we talk about death and the threat of death we are talking about something that cuts completely across age levels, class levels. It affects all of us.

In the world today 5,000 people die every hour. That is three people every two seconds. This old world we live in has to consider death whether it wants to do so or not. Our great need is to stop long enough to consider death. Moses wept for his nation. He cried for the people who simply refused to listen, saying, "Oh, that they were wise, that they understood this, that they would consider their latter end" (Deuteronomy 32:29). He was speaking of their ultimate end, their death. If we are wise, we will consider death. We go to every extreme to avoid even considering death. Our cemeteries look like everything but graveyards. They look like beautiful gardens. All are designed to take away any appearance of death. We do not even like to use the word "death" or "died." In our conversations we say things like, "Mr. Jones passed away," or "he expired." Our black friends simply say, "He passed." That is all. We dare not mention the word. We camouflage it and we shy away from it.

Listen to the Word of God on this matter. Contrary to popular thought, death is not a depressing consideration. The Bible declares that an understanding of death would not rob your life of joy. It would not cheat you. It would not cause you to have a dark outlook upon life. Instead, if we really understand what death means, it puts life and its abundancy into our experience. If we understand death, it is one of the greatest blessings in life.

We are going to have to consider death at some time. Let me show you some things the Bible says about death.

God's Word tells us that Adam lived 930 years and then died. His death has tremendous meaning for our lives, as the Apostle Paul points out.

"Wherefore, as by one man sin entered into the world, and death by sin; and so death passed upon all men, for that all have sinned: (For until the law sin was in the world: but sin is not imputed when there is no law. Nevertheless death reigned from Adam to Moses, even over them that had not sinned after the similitude of Adam's transgression, who is the figure of him that was to come. But not as the offense, so also is the free gift. For if through the offense of one many be dead, much more the grace of God, and the gift by grace, which is by one man, Jesus Christ, hath abounded unto many....) That as sin hath reigned unto death, even so might grace reign through righteousness unto eternal life by Jesus Christ our Lord" (Romans 5:12-15, 21).

This passage of Scripture reveals some very interesting and important things about death.

Certainty of Death

First of all, it emphasizes what we all ought to know and do not often accept. It stresses the certainty of death. It simply says, "...death passed upon all men." Death is life's most vivid reality. The writer of Hebrews reminds us of this certainty: "It is appointed unto a man once to die" (Hebrews 9:27). In the Old Testament, the wise woman of Tekoah addressed the king and said, "For we must need die. We are as water spilt on the ground and cannot be gathered up again" (II Samuel 14:14). James 4:13-14 provides that vivid description of life as a vapor that appears for a while and then passes away. What a description it is of the moving of life toward death.

Death is a certainty in our world. Man is appointed to die. There may be a thousand snares I have sidestepped, but someday, someway, somehow, death is going to come into my experience. Death is a certainty for each and every one of us.

Personal Nature of Death

Romans 5 also tells us that death is personal. To most of us death is just like an accident that always happens to the other person. But the Bible says that death has passed upon *all* men. You may suggest that the word "all" is a general word. I must emphasize that it is an inclusive word with terribly personal implications. When the federal government says that all of us have to pay income tax, that, too, is a very general statement. But, come April 15th each year it gets very personal. That "all" narrows down to me. It is general but it is specific. It is inclusive and it is identifying. It speaks of all men, not just in a general sense but in a personal sense. Death has a personal nature to it.

I can talk to you about the statistics of life and death and it does not bother me too much. I have learned what they are and I can relate them to you. But, when I tell you about the death of someone I know, it gets a little harder. When someone I love or someone dear to me dies, I can still relate it to you. But what really becomes difficult is to think about *my* death. I just cannot imagine the world without me! Now do not laugh, you cannot imagine a world with you. Our world revolves around us. Man is a self-conscious creature. We are conscious of ourselves. We are all aware of ourselves, and we cannot imagine the world could ever exist or get along without us. For each one of us our conscious experience with the world began when we were born and it will end when we die. And the truth of the matter is simply that someday I must die. Sooner or later I am going to face death.

I have stood at the side of many people and watched them die. I watched a man die beside the road in Central Texas some years ago. I stood by the bedside of a young man dying of a bullet wound in Kansas City, Missouri, several years ago. Here and there I have watched people die. But someday, someway, somehow I, too, shall die. Perhaps in a hospital room my loved ones will gather and they will listen as my breath grows belabored and as my chest begins to rattle with death. As my lips try to speak but cannot move and my eyes attempt to see but sight is gone, they will perhaps bend down low and someone will whisper, "Is he gone?" Yes, I must die, and my death is very personal! So, too, is your death. It is a necessity, and it is personal.

Time of Death

So, death is a certainty and it is personal. Everyone of us faces it. Everyone of us must deal with it. Well, when is it going to happen? When do we die? The truth is, we do not know. None of us knows the time of our death, but this much we can know: there is only a step between me and death. David declared this to us many years ago (I Samuel 20:3). We do not know the time or place. It could happen anywhere and at anytime. Did you know there are a thousand gates into eternity. It could happen in any experience. It could happen while you are listening to a preacher preach. While I am preaching, it could happen to me. On one trip to Virginia I discovered that the pastor of one of the largest churches in the area pronounced the benediction from his knees as he slumped to his death. There on the platform he entered a gate into eternity. Everytime I stand to preach I wonder if perhaps this is the last sermon God will let me utter. God being my witness, I want each sermon to be delivered with everything I have to offer God because it might be the last sermon I will preach.

My father died on a golf course. It occurred the first time he had taken off to play in several months. He hit the ball, walked down the fairway and died. Everytime I hit a golf ball I wonder if it will be the last time I will get to hit it. There are a thousand gates to heaven.

From where I stand, from where you sit, there is a gate straight into eternity. You may have seen that house you fondly call home for the last time. You may have kissed the lips of those whom you love and who love you for the last time. The time of death is in the hands of God. We do not know where, when or how it will overtake us.

Cause of Death

There is another aspect I want to consider with you. Have you ever wondered why people die? In this passage in Romans 5, the Apostle Paul tells us that sin is the cause. When man chose to rebel against God, man committed spiritual suicide. Sin is suicide. Sin is destructive of the very being of an individual. The truth of the Christian gospel is that if a man lives in sin, he will die eternally in his sin: "The wages of sin is death" (Romans 6:23). "Sin when it is finished bringeth forth death" (James 1:15). "The soul that sinneth it shall die" (Ezekiel 18:4). There is just one cause of death—*sin*!

If you want to get on a campaign, to demonstrate and to march, why not do it against sin? Every tear you have ever cried has been caused by sin. Every grief you have ever borne has been caused by sin. While you sin you are contributing to the death and the hell that is loose in the world today. Sin is the cause of death.

If you wonder why it is that in the most enlightened, the most intelligent, the most affluent day the world has ever known death, destruction and war are more prevalent than ever before, it is because sin is more and more in control. Sin causes death. That is why people die. That is why Paul declared, "In Adam all die" (I Corinthians 15:22). Even the Romans who had not sinned like Adam had sinned found that they were bound by death (Romans 5:14). Sin passed through Adam to the human race and death came by sin. Every time you sin, every time you rebel against God, every time you turn your heart against Him, every time you compromise, every time you turn away from God and from His will in your life, you are contributing to death in this world.

Results of Death

What happens when a person dies? What are the results of death? The result of death is quite different for the person who is an unsaved person than it is for the saved person. For the person who has rejected Christ, the one who has never given his heart personally to Jesus Christ, death means one thing. It means that you will be shut off from God and separated from peace and happiness forever.

Be assured that I am not referring to whether or not you accept theological truth. I am not referring to church membership. Nor am I discussing one's morality and ethics. If you have not had a personal encounter with Jesus Christ, a time when you have committed your life to Him, repented of your sins, and turned your life over to Him, you will be among those who are lost.

If that is your situation, let me tell you what death means for you. Death means that never again will you be bothered with the gospel message. Never again will you have to listen to a preacher preach about Jesus Christ. Never again will you see a church steeple, pointing its way to heaven and calling you to God. Never again will you hear someone appeal to you from the Word of God to give your heart to Jesus Christ. Never again will an invitation be extended to you. Never again will an arm slip around your shoulder and you be told, "I care about you." For you will have passed into darkness so dense and so dark that not even one pencil ray of hope will ever find its way to your soul. You will have closed the windows of your soul to eternity, and you will spend an eternity separated from God and separated from peace and separated from happiness. You will be lost forever.

That is exactly what it means to die without experiencing a personal faith and commitment to Jesus Christ. It shuts the door forever. You will never again be bothered with the conviction of the Holy Spirit calling you to God. You will have said, "No!" God will have said, "All right, I will leave you alone." You see, the purposes of this life are to prepare us for that which is to come. If we live in sin and death, we shall spend eternity in sin and death. If we reject Jesus Christ, we choose hell. If you want to know what hell is like, take all the turmoil, chaos, hatred, selfishness, fear, anquish and agony of this world and multiply it to infinity. That is hell. It is without limits and without bounds.

Every so often someone will say to me, "Why, I want to go to hell, because I want to be with my friends who have gone there that were not saved." Listen to me carefully! There will be millions of people in hell, but everyone of them will be *alone!* The Bible describes hell as a bottomless pit. It refers to it as outer darkness. If I had the eloquence I would attempt to describe to you how hell would be an experience of tumbling endlessly and aimlessly in a darkness so dense and so bitter that you would never see a ray of hope. Although you may be aware that others are there, you would be alone. In hell you would be cut off from all sympathy and there would be no fellowship to comfort the heart. You would be separated from God, love and hope forever. There you would be eternally alone. That is what lies in wait for you if you should die without experiencing a conversion encounter with Jesus Christ.

What about death for the Christian? In one sense, death means the same thing for the Christian ... in the sense of the opportunities of life. When a man dies the door is closed. The opportunities are over for the lost man and for the Christian alike. So, if there are some things that as a Christian I need to do, I need to do them now. It dawned upon me in the passing of my father that even to the Christian death means that I cannot do what I intended to do. The door is closed. After my father died, this was so impressed upon me that I returned home and wrote letters to everyone I could think of who had meant something to me. I wrote to my junior Sunday school teacher, my professors in college and in seminary. They must have thought I was the strangest person they had met. I wrote to say, "I want you to know I love you and I appreciate what you have meant in my life." Never before had I told them that. If there is some praise that someone is due, give it to them now before death says you cannot do it. If there is a righting that must be made between you and an individual, get it done because even for the Christian death closes the door.

Every church I have ever served has done so much more for me than I could ever have done for the church, and this is especially true with my first church. I was twenty years old and it was a little church just out of Bryan, Texas. It was such a blessing to me. In that church I had two deacons who sat on opposite sides of the church and never spoke to each other. That is probably not so bad in a large church, but in a little country church it is really noticeable. One day I was out visiting and I stopped at the home of one of those deacons. With youthful enthusiasm I broached the subject and asked, "What is the problem between you and Brother So-and-So?" And you know he told me; He really unloaded! Then I said, "Would you tell him that?" He affirmed that he would do so. I told him I would return shortly and I left. I got the chairman of the deacons and went to the home of the other deacon. I asked him to go with me to the home of the first deacon. We came back to the living room of that little country farmhouse. I asked the first deacon to tell the second deacon his complaint. You know, he did! The second deacon answered him with his side of the story. Then, we got down on our knees and prayed. I shall never forget when we got up off our knees in prayer, those two saints of God wrapped their arms around each other and tears ran down their cheeks, tears of forgiveness and restoration.

Several years later, I received a telegram that simply said, "Brother So-and-So died today." It was one of those deacons. When I received that telegram I fell to my knees and said, "Dear Jesus, thank you that this poor, naive little college preacher did not have any better sense than to get two saints of God together so that when death came they were right with each other." Even for the Christian, death closes the door. Eternity is too long to go into it angry! It is too long to go into it out-of-sorts. Can you imagine what an embarrassing situation it would be to stand before God and have some jealousy or some pettiness in my heart? How could I explain that to God? I do not want that. I am going to do everything I can right now to make sure that death does not catch me off guard. Even for the Christian death closes the door to the things we can do.

But it means more than that. For the Christian death is not a dead-end street. It is a four-lane highway. It is not an alley that dead-ends against a wall. It is an open thoroughfare that ever enlarges and deepens in its meaning, its beauty and its joy. Do I leave a home here? There is a better one over there, a house not made with hands, eternal in the heavens. Do I leave friends here? There are more friends there and better friends because they have already been perfected in Christ, and fellowship is perfect and eternity is sweet. Everything that I leave behind here I receive again there in perfection. There is a wonderful hopefulness in death. There is no despair. We do not need to fear death. The very worst that death can do is to tear down this old body in which I live and usher me into the very presence of God.

For the Christian, death need hold no fear. God is in control of our lives. Whether we live or die, we are the Lord's. We belong to Him. We are in His hands. We are not our own, we are bought with a price so let us live like it. Let us live recklessly in our world that is so cautious and in our world that is so concerned for the dollar, for prestige and for position. Let us live recklessly, knowing that we are in God's hands. We can step out on faith. We can do things for God because it is His program and it is His purposes and our lives are His.

When my father died we had a wonderful service. The soloist stood to sing, "I'll Tell the World That I'm a Christian" and "Jesus Is All I Need." The choir sang, "Have Thine Own Way, Lord," as an appeal to hearts. As the casket was rolled out of that church building, the congregation stood to sing:

> My hope is built on nothing less
> Than Jesus' blood and righteousness.
> I dare not trust the sweetest frain,
> But wholly lean on Jesus' name.
> On Christ the Solid Rock I stand,
> All other ground is sinking sand.

There was victory! Do I miss him? Yes! There are still days when the phone rings and I expect to hear him ask, "What's going on up there?" But I will tell you this. I would not bring him back if I could. He has passed the turmoil of this life. He has no more committee meetings to meet. No more pain, no more hospitals to be a patient in, and no more hurt. Because there is victory there, it adds a little spice to this life. We can live 100% of every day and still have some left over when we get to the end of the day, because we belong to Him.

The purpose of life is to prepare for that day. That is what life is all about. If you want to know why you are here, it is for you to decide what you are going to do in eternity. Every one of us has a date with death. We are all heading that way. Unless Jesus comes back again soon, every one of us is going to pass through the valley of the shadow of death. That is so for every single one of us. The purpose of life is to prepare us for that time when we receive our just deserts of death or life. "The wages of sin is death, but the gift of God is eternal life through Jesus Christ our Lord" (Romans 6:23).

Satan says to you that death is the end of it all. He encourages you to live it up. Take all you can. Withdraw everything you can from life because death is the end. God says "Not so!" God declares that death is the beginning. "If by one man's offense death reigned, much more they which receive abundance of grace and of the gift of righteousness shall reign in life by one, Jesus Christ. That as sin hath reigned unto death, even so might grace reign through righteousness unto eternal life by Jesus Christ our Lord" (Romans 5:17, 21). God says you have your choice. You can spend a little bit of time trying to live now or you can really live now and keep right on living. Jesus said, "Whosoever liveth and believeth in me shall never die" (John 11:26). There will be no more death when we get to heaven. The choice is ours. It is up to us to decide where we will spend eternity. We need to prepare for it now. In order to help us God sent His Son to die in our stead. By a faith commitment to Him we gain God's provision for eternal life in Jesus Christ. "He came unto his own, and his own received him not. But as many as received him, to them gave he power to become the sons of God, even to them that believe on his name" (John 1:11-12).

The best way to walk through life is to walk it hand in hand with the Lord of light. As S.M. Lockridge describes it, Jesus Christ walked into the grave and cleaned it out, making it a pleasant place to wait for the resurrection. He walked into the darkness of the tomb and He turned on the lights. Now we can see the way. We do not need to fear. He has walked that way before. He has gone before us and He bids us follow. The purpose of this life is to be ready for death by committing ourselves to this Jesus Christ. He has given every one of us the capacity to respond to Him. There is not one of us who has not received the God-given ability to decide for Christ, to give his life to Him. That yearning in your heart for purpose and meaning, that longing to be rid of guilt and to have forgiveness is God's spirit in you is God's way of saying, "I want to give you life." He gives life that cannot be intimidated by death. His life is eternal, and it is yours for the taking.

CHAPTER XII

Hell

As we travel along the road of life, we need to be aware that we are headed somewhere. We are going beyond this life. God has deposited inside every human being something that will transcend the boundaries of time, something that extends beyond the limits of this life. The Word of God declares that when a man passes into that other domain, which we call eternity, he will go either into heaven or hell. Heaven is a place of eternal joy and happiness, and we are elated when it is discussed. We get a little uncomfortable, however, when we read or hear about hell.

We should not be surprised to hear about hell because the Bible speaks twice as often about the judgment of God and hell as it does about heaven. The Psalmist said, "The Lord is known by the judgment which he executeth" (Psalm 9:16). Let us think for a moment. If we were to think about the ways the Lord could be known, we could list all that God has done or all that God has meant to us. We could say, "The Lord is known by the grace that he demonstrates, or by the love he shows." We believe in the grace of God and we preach the love of God, but this

Psalm does not refer to that at all. It does not say that
God is known because of His love. It does not say that the
Lord is known because of His patience. It says, "The Lord
is known because of the judgments which He executes."
God is a God of judgment.

One thing that we have never been able to understand
adequately is the fact of the holiness of God. We have
never been able to fully grasp the truth that God cannot
and will not tolerate sin. One of Satan's devices is to make
us think that God will wink at sin. Satan wants us to think
that God is not a God of wrath. He wants us to think that
God is a God of love as opposed to judgment. It is
important for us to realize that such an emphasis is a
device of Satan.

The prophet Malachi says, "Ye have wearied the Lord
with your words. Yet ye say, Wherein have we wearied
him? When ye say, Every one that doeth evil is good in
the sight of the Lord, and he delighteth in them; or,
Where is the God of judgment?" (Malachi 2:17). God says
that He has been wearied because His people have said
that good and evil are interchangeable. They have said
that the person who does evil is not going to be brought to
judgment. They have said that the person who does evil is
good in the sight of the Lord. They have fallen prey to the
device of Satan. Let us see how this is revealed by
Malachi. "Ye have said, It is vain to serve God: and what
profit is it that we have kept his ordinance, and that we
have walked mournfully before the Lord of hosts? And
now we call the proud happy; yea, they that work
wickedness are set up; yea, they that tempt God are even
delivered" (Malachi 3:14-15). The prophet declares that
one of the real tragedies of his day occurred when God's
people began to say, "God is not going to judge sin.
Those who do evil are all right. It is not so bad. God does
not really get excited about it. God is not a God of
judgment."

This is Satan's device. Look at what he told Eve back in the Garden of Eden. God had spoken to Adam and Eve and said in effect, "You have the complete run of this garden. You can go anywhere in this paradise, but there is one tree in it you should avoid. If you eat of the fruit of that tree, you will die." God had plainly said it. Now Satan came along and said, "You will not surely die. You are not going to die, Eve. God is pulling your leg. God is kidding you. He is just telling you a big one. God is not going to do that. He knows that if you eat of this tree, you are going to be as wise as God." Adam and Eve followed the lead of Satan and fell into sin. Their sin was not in eating the fruit, but it was in disobeying God. It was in rebellion against what God had told them to do. Ever since Adam and Eve took of the forbidden fruit, Satan has been saying that God does not mean what He says. Ever since that time Satan has said that God will not judge sin, that God will not punish sin. Ever since then Satan's tactic has been to tell men that there is no hell, that there is no judgment. Ever since the incident in the Garden of Eden, Satan has urged man to do everything that he can because nothing will happen. God is not going to bring judgment. The sad thing is that we have swallowed that, hook, line and sinker. There are many of us who have stayed away from Christ and have never received Him as Savior because Satan has deceived and deluded us into thinking that there will be no judgment for our sin. Many Christians have accepted the same lie. They have been deluded to believe that God is not going to bring judgment upon them for their sins.

We must understand that God tells us the truth when He says, "The Lord is known by the judgment which he executes: the wicked is snared in the work of his own hands. The wicked shall be turned into hell, and all the nations that forget God" (Psalm 9:16-17). This Psalm has a double-barreled message. When man rebels against God and stays in his sin he will be turned into hell. Every nation that turns its back upon God will have the same experience. This is what God has to say to us. This is the Word of God. This is the teaching of God for our lives.

Satan tells us that it is okay to speak about the rewards for goodness or the rewards for faith, but he does not want us to talk about what happens to a person who is separated from God. He has made many attempts to relate that God does not really mean that hell is permanent. One such attempt has resulted in the doctrine of purgatory. There is no indication anywhere in the Scriptures to support the doctrine of purgatory. It got started as an attempt to say that God would not keep man in hell throughout eternity. Let us see what the Bible reveals concerning this.

The Certainty of Hell

Let us see what the Bible says about the reality and the certainty of hell. There are at least three clear-cut reasons for the certainty of hell.

In the first place, the logic of man demands a hell. Human logic demands that we have a place of separation, a place of punishment, a hell, for those who do evil in this life. There is not a country that we know anything about that does not have some kind of punishment for those who commit crime. There is everywhere a penal system of some kind for wrongdoers. If a person cannot conform to the best interest of society, human logic demands that he be isolated and separated from society. In some way wrongdoers must be punished. If someone takes another person's life, we may argue over the degree or extent of his punishment, but we all accept the fact that he must be punished or isolated because of what he has done. Human logic demands that when a person has become an abrasive ingredient in society, whose behavior is not conductive to the best interest of society, he must be put aside.

Can you imagine what heaven would be like if everyone was there? What would heaven be like if all the criminals and vile people were there in all their fury and destructiveness? Heaven would soon stop being heaven and become a hell. Human logic tells us that those who rebel, who resist, who laugh at God, who continually break the law must be punished.

Let me show you another side of this trick of Satan when he tells us that God will not punish sin. He tells us that once we have been saved and our lives become filled with compromise that God will not take us back. He tells us God does not love us enough to restore a rebellious Christian to fellowship. Notice how he works on us. He first tells us that God loves us too much—that He will not punish us. Then he says that God will not take us back when we have sinned—that He does not love us that much. It is all a lie. Remember that we must stand upon what the Word of God says. The foundation of our hope is the Word of God. It tells us that God loves us and that He will restore us to fellowship if we will but confess our sins to Him (I John 1:9).

In the second place, the character of God demands that there be a hell. God's own character will not tolerate sin. He cannot have sin come into His presence. He is so holy that only those who are cleansed of sin can come into the perfect presence of God. Because God's character can never be compromised with sin, He demands that there be a place of eternal separation.

In the third place, Scripture confirms that there is a hell. There are numerous Scripture passages that relate God's teaching about hell. A few examples will suffice to illustrate this point.

"For a fire is kindled in mine anger, and shall burn unto the lowest hell, and shall consume the earth with her increase, and set on fire the foundations of the mountains" (Deuteronomy 32:22).

"And fear not them which kill the body, but are not able to kill the soul: but rather fear him which is able to destroy both soul and body in hell" (Matthew 10:28).

"And I say unto you, that many shall come from the east and west, and shall sit down with Abraham, and Isaac, and Jacob, in the kingdom of heaven. But the children of the kingdom shall be cast out into outer darkness; there shall be weeping and gnashing of teeth" (Matthew 8:11-12).

"The Son of man shall send forth his angels, and they shall gather out of his kingdom all things that offend, and them which do iniquity; and shall cast them into a furnace of fire: there shall be wailing and gnashing of teeth. So shall it be at the end of the world: the angels shall come forth, and sever the wicked from among the just, and shall cast them into the furnace of fire: there shall be wailing and gnashing of teeth" (Matthew 13:41-42, 49-50).

"Then shall he say also unto them on the left hand, Depart from me, ye cursed, into everlasting fire, prepared for the devil and his angels: and these shall go away into everlasting punishment: but the righteous into life eternal" (Matthew 25:41, 46).

Jesus speaking again, "And if thy hand offend thee, cut it off: it is better for thee to enter into life maimed, than having two hands to go into hell, into the fire that never shall be quenched" (Mark 9:43).

"And to you who are troubled rest with us, when the Lord Jesus shall be revealed from heaven with his mighty angels, in flaming fire taking vengeance on them that know not God, and that obey not the gospel of our Lord Jesus Christ: who shall be punished with everlasting destruction from the presence of the Lord, and from the glory of his power" (II Thessalonians 1:7-9).

"For if God spared not the angels that sinned, but cast them down to hell, and delivered them into chains of darkness, to be reserved unto judgment...the Lord knoweth how to deliver the godly out of temptations, and to reserve the unjust unto the day of judgment to be punished'' (II Peter 2:4, 9).

"And the angels which kept not their first estate, but left their own habitation, he hath reserved in everlasting chains under darkness unto the judgment of the great day. Even as Sodom and Gomorrha, and the cities about them in like manner, giving themselves over to fornication, and going after strange flesh, are set forth for an example, suffering the vengeance of eternal fire'' (Jude 6-7).

"And the smoke of their torment ascendeth up for ever and ever: and they have not rest day nor night, who worship the beast and his image, and whosoever receiveth the mark of his name'' (Revelation 14:11).

Then we can turn again to our original passage, "The Lord is known for the judgments that he executeth. The wicked shall be turned into Hell and all nations that forget God'' (Psalm 9:16-17).

All these Scripture passages underscore the doctrine of hell and eternal punishment as a key and cardinal doctrine of the Word of God. We can deny it if we like, but we will deny it over the Word of God. It is very plain. There is a place of eternal punishment and separation for all those who rebel against God. Human logic demands it. God's character demands it. The Scriptures confirm it.

The Circumstances of Hell

What are the circumstances of hell? What is it like? The Bible describes hell as a lake of fire. Now, I do not know if it is literally a place of fire. I do know, I never was afraid of a picture of fire, but when I am in a real fire I am scared to death. If the Bible picture of hell is just symbolic, if fire is just a picture, it is the most horrible description that I have ever heard in my life. Imagine, if the symbol is so severe, what is the real thing like? I do not know because I have never been to hell. I do know this, I know the Word of God says that hell is a place of fire. Now that is what the Word of God says, and I am willing to take God's Word for it. I do not want to check it out for myself. I believe God when He said it is a place of fire.

The Bible also teaches that hell is an eternal abode. The verses we have read underscore the fact that when we pass through the valley of the shadow of death, we do not have an instant replay on life. We never have a rerun. We never have a second chance once we pass through death into eternity. If we die without Christ, we will go into an eternal separation from God. There is no changing the fact that our fate is sealed. It is eternal.

In addition, hell is a rational experience. We are told in the Word of God, that the man in hell sees, he thinks, he knows, he remembers, he cries, he weeps, he does all of these things that a rational human being can do. We know that there will not be an insanity that will pass upon the mind to free men from the horrors of hell. It is a rational experience.

It is the experience of forever dying. It is called "eternal death." Have you ever been with someone when they died? I do not just mean someone who slipped into eternity, I mean someone who struggled with life. I mean someone whose body was in the throes of death, where there was a struggle to keep the body from being separated from life. The Bible says that hell is going to be a place where men are always in the process of dying, but then never die. Their experience is one of separation and struggle where they wish they could just die and get it all finished. The Book of the Revelation relates a song of agony where men cried for the rocks and the mountains to fall on them, to hide them and take their lives and take them out of the judgment that had befallen them. But death never comes in hell. Man is always dying but never being able to die.

Hell was previewed for us in the cross of Christ. If you want to know what hell is like, just look at the cross. There you can see Jesus Christ whose soul, emotions and heart were pressed upon by the weight of sin. His agony was indescribable. As He died upon the cross in the middle of the day, a sudden blackness of midnight swallowed up the earth and the earth began to rock and to reel. Nature revolted at the weight of sin as it pressed upon Jesus. In that instability, graves shook and tombstones fell and the dead came out of their graves. What a terrifying experience. Hell was previewed in the cross. The death of Christ upon the cross tells us how badly God wants us to avoid going to hell. He loved us so much that He gave His only Son to keep us from spending eternity in separation from Him. Oh, how God wants us to be free from the ravages of hell!

Hell is also seen in the agony of this world. Think for a moment of all the hell in this world. Everything that we fear—the turmoil of our minds, the guilt that we bear so often, the depression, the discouragement, the poverty, the war, the fear, the hatred, everything that we do not want in this world is an expression of the circumstances of hell. Think about it for a moment. Now think about those things amassed and accumulated in intensity so that they fall on you without restraint. Then imagine that situation expanded into seeming infinity. That is hell. It is seen in the agony of this world. Everything that is bad about this world is going to be magnified and intensified forever in the experience of hell.

Well, just what kind of a place is hell? Hell has some of the same characteristics as heaven. Heaven is a place—so is hell. It is a real place. Heaven is a place prepared for individuals who choose to go there—so is hell. Hell is a place prepared for those who reject God. It is a place for those who choose to be their own gods, to dictate their own lives, to ruin their own lives. In that sense, it has some of the same characteristics as heaven.

Neverless, hell is the opposite of heaven in many ways. Heaven is a beautiful place, but hell is just the opposite. Hell is the most horrible place you can ever imagine. All the viciousness, the hatred, the selfishness, and all the other things we feel are ugly about this world are only foretastes of what hell is like. Heaven is beautiful, but hell is an ugly, horrifying place. There is no separation in heaven, but there is separation in hell. I have had people to tell me that they want to go to hell so they can be with their parents. Let me tell you something. If they are there and you are there, you will not be together. You will not see them. You and they will be experiencing such agony and isolation that you will not even be concerned about them. Hell is a place where people will suffer alone. There may be millions of people there, but they will never comfort one another. They will not experience the privilege of companionship. They will be totally alone.

Heaven is a place where there will be no darkness, hell is a place where there will be no light. If you can imagine falling into a deep, dark, pit, constantly turning and rolling and falling, hearing cries of other people, knowing that they are there, but never seeing them, never touching them, never communicating with them—that is what hell is like. Its inhabitants are going to be alone in the depths of darkness and in a darkness so dense that not even one pencil-ray of hope will ever come to them. There will never be a comforting word spoken to them. There will never be a hand placed upon a shoulder or someone to say, "I care about you." The inhabitants of hell will be absolutely separated for all eternity. All alone, their experience will be just the opposite of those in heaven.

Heaven is a place where there will be no tears, but hell is a place where there are rivers of tears. There will be great weeping, wailing and the gnashing of teeth in great sorrow. Have you ever gnashed your teeth? We never gnash our teeth unless we are in severe pain. Gnashing the teeth is something that is associated with a terrifying and excruciating pain. Heaven has no pain, but in hell there is pain like this world has never seen, where gnashing of teeth is perpetual. There will be weeping, wailing, and gnashing of teeth to a degree we have never imagined. It will be just the opposite of heaven.

There will be no poverty in heaven, but that will be all there is in hell. Want, poverty, deprivation and need will never be satisfied in hell. There will never be a satisfaction of need. There will never be any relief of pain. There will never be any help to get release for individuals in hell. There will only be poverty, misery, pain and loneliness in hell. Life there will be just one big, empty need without relief or satisfaction. When we go to be with the Lord in heaven, there will be no more curse, but there will be nothing but the curse in hell. That is all that there is there. All of the curse of this world will pass into an eternal hell. Again, hell is the opposite of heaven.

Heaven is a place of worship. It is because God is there. God will not be in hell. Since He will never be there, there will be no worship of Him there. There will never be an opportunity for the inhabitants of hell to experience worship, because worship cannot be had until we encounter God. We cannot worship God if He is not there. Those who will spend eternity in hell, are going to be in a place where God will never be. God will not be there—ever! As a result, we could not worship Him as God if we were in hell. Imagine that, everything we have ever longed to experience in heaven will be denied in hell. What a terrible experience it would be for us to go to hell.

The Crowds of Hell

Who is going to hell? What about the crowds of people who will be in hell? The Bible tells us, "Know ye not that the unrighteous shall not inherit the kingdom of God? Be not deceived: neither fornicators, nor idolaters, nor adulterers, nor effeminate, nor abusers of themselves with mankind, nor thieves, nor covetous, nor drunkards, nor revilers, nor extortioners, shall inherit the kingdom of God" (I Corinthians 6:9-10). In another passage we are told, "But the fearful, and unbelieving, and the abominable, and murderers, and whoremongers, and sorcerers, and idolaters, and all liars, shall have their part in the lake which burneth with fire and brimstone: which is the second death" (Revelation 21:8). It goes on to say, "And whosoever was not found written in the book of life was cast into the lake of fire" (Revelation 20:15).

Well, just who is going to be in hell? If you and I are honest, we will see ourselves named in one of those lists. I stayed off the list when it named sorcerers, idolaters, whoremongers and effeminate persons. But when it got down to liars, etc., the list included me, because the charge hit me between the eyes. Do not be self-righteous, because when you are, you become a liar too. You see, we are all named in those lists somewhere. The question is, how are we going to stay out of hell and get into heaven?

The Bible says, "And whosoever was not found written in the book of life was cast into the lake of fire" (Revelation 20:15). Those who go to hell are the very ones who refuse to allow Christ to bear their sins. When Jesus Christ died on the cross, he bore the sins of every person who will ever live. He bore the sin of adultery, he bore the sin of lying, he bore the sin of dishonesty, cheating, murder, idolatry, hatred and the likes upon the cross. You and I can choose to pay for our sins again if we so desire.

We can do it by rejecting Jesus Christ. The result will be spending eternity in hell. But, if we accept Jesus Christ as our provision, He will write our names in the Book of Life, and His death will be sufficient payment for our sins.

Everyone who has turned his back on Christ is going to spend eternity in hell. It matters not what else we may be or do. It matters not how good we try to be. The decision to accept or reject Christ's provision is the determining factor. Now there are some people, I feel, who ought to go to hell. I really do not have any trouble invisioning them in hell at all. Take someone like a terrible murderer for instance. He played God with people's lives and many people were killed because he was playing God. I do not have any trouble seeing someone like that in hell. Do you? I do not have any trouble seeing how someone who is filled with hate and whose life is used to destroy is going to spend eternity in hell.

But let me tell you what bothers me somewhat. Take the sweet, fine neighbor I have. He is gracious, kind, thoughtful and concerned. He is good, honest and does his best to do good to those about him. But, if he does not give his life to Christ, he, too, is going to hell. Even those wonderful husbands or sweet wives whom I see in various homes, they, too, are good and kind, but they do not know Jesus Christ as Savior. The Bible identifies those who are destined to hell as "the unbelieving" (Revelation 21:8). To refuse to believe in Jesus Christ is just as vicious a sin against God as it is to be a murderer, an idolator, or anything else. If we have not been guilty of any of the great sins that we call social sins, but we have been guilty of unbelief, we are deserving of hell even now. Those unbelievers are the ones who are going to be in hell. Those who have disbelieved God, those who have not received what God offers to them, will spend their eternity cut off from God because of their unbelief.

The Contrast of Hell

Now I would like to show the contrast, the change that is caused by Jesus Christ. Paul speaks of all the vicious sins, of the pagan and heathen worshippers of false gods. As he lists those great and grievous sins, he adds, "Among whom also we all had our conversation in times past in the lusts of our flesh, fulfilling the desires of the flesh and of the mind; and were by nature the children of wrath, even as others. But God, who is rich in mercy, for his great love wherewith he loved us, even when we were dead in sins, hath quickened us together with Christ, (by grace ye are saved;) and hath raised us up together, and made us sit together in heavenly places in Christ Jesus: that in the ages to come he might shew the exceeding riches of this grace in his kindness toward us through Christ Jesus" (Ephesians 2:3-7). That is the contrast of which I am speaking. None of us ought to go to heaven because every one of us has earned a place in hell. When we stand before God, we do not want justice, we want mercy. If we got justice, we would spend eternity in hell. We do not deserve salvation. Not one of us deserves it, and that is the miracle and the amazing thing about the love of God. We, who deserve hell, are going to make heaven our eternal destiny because of Jesus Christ. We, who deserve to spend eternity separated from God, are going to spend eternity in perfect unity with God because of what Jesus Christ has done for us and on our behalf.

If we go to hell we will go over the dead body of Jesus Christ. We will go over His broken body. We will spend eternity in hell in spite of what He has done, and because of our unbelief and self-will. When Jesus Christ was nailed to the cross nearly 2000 years ago, that cross was erected in the center of the broad road that deads to eternal hell, to eternal destruction. It was erected at the center of that path that leads every man to hell. On that cross, Jesus cried out, "Stop! Watch what you do! Take

my provision for your sin. Stop, before it is too late.''
What that means is this: Jesus wants to stop us. He does
not want us to go to hell. He does not want us to live in
hell apart from God for all eternity. He wants to free us
from our isolation, misery, and hopelessness. The only
thing that will keep us from receiving His provision is our
own refusal. That is all. The only thing that keeps us from
knowing God, experiencing the forgiveness of our sins,
and having a place reserved for us in heaven, is our
refusal to accept Jesus Christ.

God's invitation is for us to receive eternal life through
His Son, Jesus Christ. Settle the issue. Do not choose to
spend eternity in hell, separated from God. Invite Him
into your life now and prepare for real life for all eternity.

CHAPTER XIII

The Coming King

Surely we stand on the brink of the most tremendous and fantastic experience that the world will ever see. Nearly two thousand years ago, God invaded human history. He came in the Person of Jesus Christ. After His crucifixion and resurrection, Jesus Christ ascended again into heaven. On that occasion He told those gathered around Him that He would come back to the earth again in bodily form. In order to help His followers understand what His coming is going to be, He left directions about the signs of His return. We can see these signs as they are fulfilled in our day. In fact, in recent days we have seen repeated examples of fulfilled prophecy printed in the daily news. When the Word of God speaks about the Second Coming of Christ, it seems to be as current as today's newspaper. What an exciting, wonderful, and relevant truth it is. Jesus Christ is going to come again.

Space does not permit us to go through the hundreds of passages in the Bible that related to the Second Coming. There are 330 of them in the New Testament alone. Twenty-three of the twenty-seven books in the New Testament deal with the Second Coming. It is a tremendous truth of the Word of God. Here is just one example of a passage on the Second Coming of Jesus. "For the Lord himself shall descend from heaven with a shout, with the voice of the archangel, and with the trump of God: and the dead in Christ shall rise first: Then we which are alive and remain shall be caught up together with them in the clouds to meet the Lord in the air: and so shall we ever be with the Lord" (I Thessalonians 4:16-17). Matthew 24 describes the Lord's return as the lightning that dances across the sky on a stormy night. Just as the lightning darts across the sky and illuminates the darkened night, so quickly will be His return in the clouds of the sky. What a tremendous revelation. The King is coming. The Word of God tells it plainly. It tells us that Jesus Christ will return to the earth and reveal Himself again to man. Yes, He will make another appearance on the earth to establish His reign, but some things must occur before that great kingdom is established.

Reasons for His Coming

First of all, sin has to be punished. We are living in a world of nightmares. Things are just not right. There are injustices. There are atrocities. There are things that we know should not be. There is disease, war, fear, hatred and death. These things should not be, but we know they exist. They are the result of sin, and God is not going to allow sin to go unpunished. God is going to bring a day when He will deal with sin. He will judge it, punish it, and release the earth from its grip. "And the kings of the earth, and the great men, and the rich men, and the chief captains, and the mighty men, and every bondman, and every free man, hid themselves in the dens and in the rocks of the mountains; and said to the mountains and rocks, Fall on us, and hide us from the face of him that sitteth on the throne, and from the wrath of the Lamb; for the great day of his wrath is come; and who shall be able to stand?'' (Revelation 6:15-17).

The writer of Jude says, ''Behold, the Lord cometh with ten thousands of his saints, to execute judgment upon all, and to convince all that are ungodly among them of all their ungodly deeds which they have ungodly committed, and of all their hard speeches which ungodly sinners have spoken against him'' (Jude 14-15). Look at the word ''ungodly'' in this passage. It is a very strong word and it is used three times in this brief verse. God is angry about sin. He is not going to put up with it. He is going to judge the ungodly for their deeds. Then He will lift the curse upon the earth. ''For all creation is waiting patiently and hopefully for that future day when God will resurrect his children. For on that day thorns and thistles, sin, death and decay—the things that overcame the world against its will at God's command—will all disappear, and the world around us will share in the glorious freedom from sin which God's children enjoy'' (Romans 8:19-21—*Living Bible*). There is coming a day when God is going to make right all the wrong that has brought a curse upon this earth and its inhabitants.

Now, you say, ''I cannot wait that long, because there have been so many wrongs and so much suffering for so long a time.'' Let me say to you that the wrongs and the atrocities of this world have been brief in their duration. Not only that, very soon now, they will all have become past tense. The Bible says that the days of this earth are like the time it takes for an arrow to leave its bow and strike its target. All history is but a brief period when compared with eternity. Eternity is forever.

Some may have laughed at God and have said, ''Aha, I have gotten away with all the things I have tried. Yes, I have put one over on God.'' Just remember that God does not pay off all His debts when we think He will. A day is coming when God will sit in judgment over this earth. On that occasion, God will judge and punish sin. If you question that, I would take you back for a moment to Calvary. There God allowed His son to die in order to demonstrate the fact that He will not tolerate sin. If God could tolerate sin in any way, Jesus never would have had to come, to suffer and to die for it. But Jesus suffered and died in ridicule as a criminal. Though He had no sin in Him, He bore all sin upon Himself. That is the length to which God went to correct sin and its penalty. He cannot tolerate it at all. One day He is going to send His son to the earth again to punish sin.

In addition, the earth has to be restored. When Jesus Christ came to earth in His first advent, the earth received Him. When He told the fish to get into a net, they got into the net. When He told the loaves to multiply, they multiplied. When He told the wind to stop blowing, it stopped blowing. When He told the rain to stop falling, it stopped falling. When He told the sea to become calm, it became calm. The creation obeyed Jesus Christ and was ready to receive Him. But man refused and rejected Jesus Christ and, as our passage in Romans eight tells us, the judgment of God for sin fell upon this created world. It still groans and travails under the bondage of sin. One day a time will come when the lion and the lamb will lie down together. Someday we will be able to pluck a rose and not find a thorn on its stem. The time will come when even a snake will not be a threat. It has to happen. It is in God's design, for the whole creation awaits God's judgment of sin. "For the whole creation groaneth and travaileth in pain together until now" (Romans 8:22). The King will come to free this old world, the creation itself, from the curse and bondage of sin.

More than that, the godly must be rewarded. The Bible says, "Unto him that loved us, and washed us from our sins in his own blood, and hath made us kings and priests unto God and his Father; to him be glory and dominion for ever and ever" (Revelation 1:5-6). That has not happened yet, but God has promised a day for such reward. Have you ever wondered why the good guys seem to finish last so much? Have you ever wondered why good people suffer? Have you ever wondered why the unfairness of this world seems to be meted out to the innocent? It is because of sin. In order to correct that, Jesus Christ must come and reward those who have given themselves to God.

On a day, Simon Peter asked Jesus, "What are we going to get out of following you?" Jesus did not say, "Shame on you, Simon, you are looking out for yourself and you should not be concerned about that." Instead, He said, "Anyone who gives up his home, brothers, sisters, father, mother, wife, children, or property, to follow me, shall receive a hundred times as much in return, and shall have eternal life" (Matthew 19:29 —*Living Bible*). An hundredfold is 10,000 per cent interest. That is why I like to give money to the Lord's work. God is going to pay me 10,000 per cent interest on it. I do not know how it is going to be transferred into the treasury of heaven, but I know that when I give it to Him, it is laid up as treasures in heaven where God is keeping accounts and giving the interest. A day is coming when the godly will be rewarded. Jesus Christ must come in order for that to happen.

Finally, Jesus Christ must come in order for all mankind to crown Him King of kings and Lord of lords. "Wherefore God also hath highly exalted him, and given him a name which is above every name: that at the name of Jesus every knee should bow, of things in heaven, and things in earth, and things under the earth; and that every tongue should confess that Jesus Christ is Lord, to the glory of God the Father" (Philippians 2:9-11). Some day every tongue is going to confess that Jesus Christ is Lord to the glory of God the Father. It is appointed to be on the clock of God. The Book of the Revelation speaks of this in boldness: "The kingdoms of this world are become the kingdoms of our Lord, and of his Christ; and he shall reign for ever and ever" (Revelation 11:15). The Old Testament says that God is going to give Jesus the throne in Jerusalem (Isaiah 9:6-7). That has not yet happened. But it is going to happen. He is going to be crowned King of kings and Lord of lords. He is going to reign as King of this earth and King of all eternity. He will be seated in Jerusalem. In order for Him to be crowned King, He must come again.

Events at His Coming

When Jesus comes again there will be a sequence of events that will transpire. The first of these is that the saints are going to be taken out of this world. That will occur in two parts virtually simultaneously. The dead in Christ will rise first (I Thessalonians 4:16). What a wonderful time that will be. The dead in Christ will stir from their graves and rise to meet the Lord in the air. There will be a disturbance in the cemetery when Jesus says, "Get up!" Every believer who has ever been put into the ground, every believer who has ever been cremated, though his ashes may have been swept to the four winds, every believer whose body has ever settled beneath the waters of the sea, is going to rise to meet the Lord in the air. The Spirit of God will pull the decay of those bones and flesh back together again. Bone upon bone and marrow upon marrow, each believer will be clothed in a body that is an eternal body. Each will receive a glorified body when they go to meet Jesus in the air. This is to be a meeting "in the air" with living believers. The graves are going to open. The dead in Christ are going to be raised and transformed. They are going to meet the Lord in the air.

While that is going on, living Christians are going to be caught up to meet them in the air. "Then we which are alive and remain shall be caught up together with them in the clouds to meet the Lord in the air: and so shall we ever be with the Lord" (I Thessalonians 4:17). What an exciting time! We are going to rise. We are going to be taken out of the earth. When the church is taken out, the stage will be set for terrible tribulation. Jesus said, "For then shall be great tribulation, such as was not since the beginning of the world to this time, no, nor ever shall be" (Matthew 24:21). It will be so terrifying that words fail in their attempt to describe it. It is going to be triggered by the fact that Christians are going to taken out of the world.

The removal of the church will set off a chain reaction of tribulation events. It will be a time of terrible tribulation. Today Christians are the salt of the earth. They are keeping evil from running rampant. If we think things are bad now, just wait. The Holy Spirit is now present in the world. He indwells Christians at this time in history. The Holy Spirit is also dealing with the hearts of men. He is a restraining influence in the world. When the Holy Spirit and the church are gone, evil will run rampant in the earth. Then a time of great tribulation will commence.

The Time of His Coming

Some things really excite me as I realize the nearness of the coming of the Lord. (My excitement was first kindled as I listened to Dr. Bill Stewart of Moody Bible Institute share some of these concepts.) We stand today in the first age that has ever dawned, the first generation that has ever lived upon this earth when Jesus could return. This conclusion is based upon what He has very plainly revealed to us in His Word. He has given to us the key to unlock the mystery of His return. That key is the Middle

East, and its turning in the lock of history is what has happened to Israel in the past and what is happening to Israel today.

In the past, Israel was scattered. God prophesied that they would be scattered because of their rebellion against Him. "If you refuse to obey all the laws written in this book, thus refusing reverence to the glorious and fearful name of Jehovah your God, then Jehovah will send perpetual plagues upon you and upon your children. Just as the Lord has rejoiced over you and has done such wonderful things for you and has multiplied you, so the Lord at that time will rejoice in destroying you; and you shall disappear from the land. For the Lord will scatter you among all the nations from one end of the earth to the other" (Deuteronomy 28:59, 63-64 —*Living Bible*). This was spoken to Moses before the Israelites had arrived in the land which God promised them. They had not even possessed the land. Nevertheless, God said, "For the Lord will scatter you among all the nations from one end of the earth to the other. There you will worship heathen gods that neither you nor your ancestors have known, gods made of wood and stone! There among those nations you shall find no rest, but the Lord will give you trembling hearts, darkness, and bodies wasted from sorrow and fear. Your lives will hang in doubt. You will live night and day in fear, and will have no reason to believe that you will see the morning light" (Deuteronomy 28:64-66).

What a picture of God's chosen people! If there were ever people of failing hearts and trembling eyes, if there were ever people whose lives hung in doubt before them, surely it is this people. Look at what the Bible says about them. "In the morning you will say, 'Oh, that night were here!' And in the evening you will say, 'Oh, that morning were here!' You will say this because of the awesome horror surrounding you" (Deuteronomy 28:67—*Living Bible*).

In essence God said to Moses, "These people you are leading are going to possess the land I promised to them. But the day is going to come when I am going to pluck them off the land and I am going to scatter them all over the world. They are going to be afraid for their lives. Everywhere they go, they will have no ease, no rest." We do not even have to be casual historians to know that this has been the lot of the Jewish nation. Only in America have Jews found any semblance of rest. Even here it appears that they have not found much rest. "Through all the years of history," God said, "I am going to scatter them." That has happened. For 2500 years the Jews have been scattered all over the earth, in every nation.

On May 14, 1948, Israel was formed as an independent nation for the first time in over 2500 years. Although there had been Jews throughout all those centuries, now, for the first time, the nation Israel was independent and able to direct its own destiny. That has happened within the last 27 years. It has happened in our lifetime. We have seen it take place.

Now that raises a question. Why are the Jews going back to the Middle East? Why, all of a sudden, are they returning to their former homeland? They are returning so fast that the area appears to have exploded. Jerusalem is now a city of about 200,000 people and predictions are that within a very short time it will have more than 900,000 people. The land of Israel is virtually exploding with population as Jewish people pour in from all over the world. But why are they returning? The Bible provides us the answer in the prophecy of Jeremiah. "Thus speaketh the Lord God of Israel, saying, Write thee all the words that I have spoken unto thee in a book. For, lo, the days come, saith the Lord, that I will bring again the captivity of my people Israel and Judah, saith the Lord: and I will cause them to return to the land that I gave to their fathers, and they shall possess it" (Jeremiah 30:2-3).

According to Jeremiah, God is causing Israel to return. He goes on to provide the reason for their return as being for a great confrontation between Israel and the forces of Satan. He adds, "Alas! for that day is great, so that none is like it: it is even the time of Jacob's trouble, but he shall be saved out of it" (Jeremiah 30:7). The time of Jacob's trouble is synonymous with the tribulation period of God's timetable. Throughout the Old Testament there is reference to the time of Jacob's trouble. It refers to the time when Israel will suffer a great and terrible tribulation. "But, first," God says, "I will cause the people to return, then there will be a time of tribulation."

Following that time of tribulation they will be converted to Jesus Christ. Then, "They shall serve the Lord their God, and David their king, whom I will raise up unto them. I will save thee from afar, and thy seed from the land of their captivity; and Jacob shall return, and shall be in rest, and be quiet, and none shall make him afraid" (Jermiah 30:9-10).

Now, there are three important things in this description by Jeremiah. First, God says, "I will cause them to return." Then he says, "There will be a time of terrible tribulation." Finally, he says, "It will be a saving time. I will bring them in so they will be converted and serve me. I will be their God." As we look at those events going on in the world today, it makes us think that we are in the midst of the first step mentioned by Jeremiah. God is causing Israel to return. In their spiritual blindness, they do not even know why. God is doing it. He is causing them to return even though they do not understand it. Much study is going on now in the Jewish University in Jerusalem to try to understand what is happening to the Jewish people and nation. Even Christian scholars are being brought in by the government to study biblical prophecy in an attempt to understand. They know something is causing them to return. This is the first step in Jeremiah's prophecy, and God is causing it to happen.

There is tension in the Middle East as spoken of by Zechariah in the Old Testament. "I will make Jerusalem and Judah like a cup of poison to all the nearby nations that send their armies to surround Jerusalem. Jerusalem will be a heavy stone burdening the world. And though all the nations of the earth unite in an attempt to move her, they will all be crushed" (Zechariah 12:2-3—*Living Bible*). God promises that there will be a day when the nation called Israel will arise and become the center of controversy. God promises that Israel will be something of a political "hot potato." Israel will cause confusion and problems. It will be a terrible burden to its neighbors. It will be a sore spot. It will be troublesome.

That time spoken of by Zechariah has come to pass. Israel is the center of frustration to her neighbors. Israel is the focal point of disturbance among all nations. This description was penned thousands of years ago. Zechariah said it would involve all the nations surrounding it, and that this would spread to include all nations. It is no wonder that there are problems in the Middle East. There can never be peace in the Middle East in this age. God said that peace will not come to the nation Israel there. God's Word tells us that we can try every possible solution, but we will not solve the problem. Israel in the Middle East is a problem whose solution is beyond the capabilities of man. The United Nations Security Council has not yet settled even one matter relative to Israel. Every issue involving Israel has been tabled and unsettled. That body has never been able to solve the problem of Israel in the Middle East. That is exactly what God said years before there was ever a United Nations formed! God said that the Middle East will be the focal point of struggle and turmoil, and the entire Middle East is like a powder keg awaiting the charge that will cause it to explode.

In June of 1967 Israel defeated the Arabic nations in a short, six-day war. 250,000 Israeli soldiers went against the armies of 114,000,000 people, and they won! The very existence of Israel today is a miracle of God,...and one prophesied by God centuries before. Yet, the scene is one of tension and struggle. As God promised it is an explosive situation.

The Bible further declares that after the establishment of the nation of Israel that there will come a change in the form of government. This change in the form of government must take place before there will be ultimate confrontation between Russia and Egypt and the people of Israel. The Bible is very clear that in this new Israel there will be a king for the nation. Many think that this king will be the antichrist. Israel will be defeated by Russia and Egypt, but she must have a king first. Daniel's prophecy tells us of the coming to power of this king. It speaks of the way he will make promises to gain power through deception. Daniel is very descriptive. "And some of them of understanding shall fall, to try them, and to purge, and to make them white, even to the time of the end: because it is yet for a time appointed. And the king shall do according to his will; and he shall exalt himself, and magnify himself above every god, and shall speak marvelous things against the God of gods, and shall prosper till the indignation be accomplished; for that that is determined shall be done. Neither shall he regard the God of his fathers, nor the desire of women, nor regard any god: for he shall magnify himself above all" (Daniel 11:35-37).

Israel does not now have a king, but one day soon she will. God works his plan "for a time appointed." All things come about according to God's timetable. In 1948, in order to get the United Nations to agree to establish the nation of Israel, they agreed to have a democratic form of government. They agreed that any Arab who chose to stay in Israel could be a citizen. Thousands of Arabs became citizens of Israel. Perhaps it is these Arab citizens of Israel who will force the change in Israel's governmental form. At any rate, Israel will have a single ruler, perhaps even a king, certainly a dictator of some kind.

From April to October, 1968, Dr. Robert Moskin had a series of articles in *Look* magazine. In those articles, the author, a Jewish scholar, squarely and honestly faced the problems I am discussing. He said that Israel's real problems lie with the Arabs "inside" Israel. Their birth rate is far greater than the Jewish birth rate. Because of this, within twenty years there will be more voting Arabs in Israel than voting Jews. That means that within approximately twenty years from 1968, the Arabs in Israel could vote to oust the Jews from power in Israel. Do you think that is going to happen? Do you think the Jews are going to turn loose of what they have sought for more than 2500 years? Do you think they are going to let the democratic process keep them from having control over their land? No! Absolutely not! They will do anything to keep that from happening.

Well, what is the answer? Moskin explored the possible solutions in his series of articles. He suggested that Israel will change its form of government from a democracy to a monarchy to cope with the problem. Then Israel will again have a king. They will do it because they will need to have a society where no one can vote. If they kick the Arabs out of Israel, the rest of the world will condemn them, and they will have betrayed their trust with the United Nations. The only alternative for Israel is to have a king. Even the Israeli appraisal of the role of the Arabs in Israel points to that solution. It could come about within twenty years from 1968.

Now, all these things will happen in the last day. There will be a great confrontation between Israel, led by her king, and her enemies. "And at the time of the end shall the king of the south push at him: and the king of the north shall come against him like a whirlwind, with chariots, and with horsemen, and with many ships; and he shall enter into the countries, and shall overflow and pass over. He shall enter also into the glorious land" (Daniel 11:40-41).

Have you wondered why Russia and Egypt have not already conquered Israel? They made an alliance in 1949. At this very time, the largest naval armada that has ever been assembled is sitting in the Mediterranean Sea just one mile outside the territorial limits of Israel. It belongs to the Soviet Union. Why have they not moved against Israel? They have not moved because God has not permitted it. It is not the appropriate time on God's timetable. God has said that they cannot move against Israel until Israel has a king.

Just when will God give permission for this to transpire? He tells us in the New Testament. "Now we beseech you, brethren, by the coming of our Lord Jesus Christ, and by our gathering together unto him, that ye be not soon shaken in mind, or be troubled, neither by spirit, nor by word, nor by letter as from us, as that the day of Christ is at hand. Let no man deceive you by any means: for that day shall not come, except there come a falling away first, and that man of sin be revealed, the son of perdition" (II Thessalonians 2:1-3). Nearly every modern Bible and biblical interpreter translates this expression as "falling away." I do not believe that is what it means. The Greek word is *apostasia*. *Apostasia* comes from a root word that can be translated "falling away." As such we get our English word "apostasy" from this Greek word. It can also be translated as "a going away," or "a taking away." It is so translated in many Greek writings. I do not know why the translators have chosen to make it appear that this is an apostasy where people forsake the faith. Perhaps that is the case, but I believe the Apostle Paul is speaking of the rapture. He says there is going to be "a going away." "That day will not come except there come a going away and then the man of sin be revealed." The man of sin is the King. He is the king, "Who opposeth and exalteth himself above all that is called God, or that is worshipped; so that he as God sitteth in the temple of God, showing himself that he is God" (II Thessalonians 2:4).

The two things that must happen before Israel will be conquered by Russia and the time of tribulation comes are the saints must be taken away and Israel must have a king. God works on a timetable. His plan has an omniscient design behind it. "Don't you remember that I told you this when I was with you? And you know what is keeping him from being here already; for he can come only when his time is ready. As for the work this man of rebellion and hell will do when he comes, it is already going on, but he himself will not come until the one who is holding him back steps out of the way" (II Thessalonians 2:5-7— *Living Bible*). Centuries before the Holy Spirit came on the Day of Pentecost, God said it would take place. Then, when God's purpose was ready the Holy Spirit came at the appointed time. God's Word says that Jesus came "in the fulness of time" (Galatians 4:4). He came at the split-second that God intended. When we look toward the second coming of Christ, we must remember that God is still working on a time schedule. Christ will come in God's time.

Have you ever wondered about the one who is holding him back? I believe Him to be the Holy Spirit. He now permits what is taking place. He intervenes and directs the course of events. He is the preservative in our society. One day He is going to be taken away and, "then this wicked one will appear" (II Thessalonians 2:8 —*Living Bible*). The Holy Spirit will not permit Israel to have a king while He is working in the world. The Holy Spirit must leave before Israel can have a king. He cannot leave without us, the church. Our Lord promised that when He said, "I will pray the Father, and he shall give you another Comforter, that he may abide with you for ever" (John 14:16). The Holy Spirit will never leave the saints. He cannot leave without taking the saints with Him. This is called "the rapture" of the saints. The rapture occurs before the last great conflict of Russia and Egypt against Israel. It cannot happen until Israel has a king, and that cannot happen until the Holy Spirit is gone—and He cannot leave without us. It is as simple as that. That is the sequence of events as they move along God's timetable. That is what we are facing in the world today. The dead in Christ will soon be raised. Jesus spoke of all these things when he said, "This generation (the generation that is alive when these things begin to happen) shall not pass, till all these things be fulfilled" (Matthew 24:34).

The Word of God plainly reveals to us that we are living in the last days. Jesus can come again because the conditions are right. God is working according to His great timetable. These things must take place. The church will be taken away and then Israel will have a king. Then in that land that is only 50 miles wide and about 200 miles long, will be the place where history will draw to its dramatic climax. It is unfolding before our very eyes. Since Israel must have a king before Russia and Egypt can move against her, since none of this can happen until the Holy Spirit is taken out of the world, and since He cannot go without taking the believers with Him, how soon our going must be. Are you ready?